DATE DUE

#47-0108 Peel Off Pressure Sensitive

President Lincoln in 1861
From a photograph given by him to Julia Taft

Tad Lincoln's Father

Julia Taft Bayne

INTRODUCTION TO THE BISON BOOKS EDITION BY

Mary A. DeCredico

UNIVERSITY OF NEBRASKA PRESS

Lincoln and London

Introduction © 2001 by the University of Nebraska Press
Manufactured in the United States of America

⊗

First Bison Books printing: 2001

Library of Congress Cataloging-in-Publication Data
Bayne, Julia Taft, 1845–1933.
Tad Lincoln's father / by Julia Taft Bayne.
p. cm.
ISBN 0-8032-6191-8 (pbk. : alk. paper)
1. Lincoln, Abraham, 1809–1865.   2. Lincoln, Abraham, 1809–1865—Family.   3. Lincoln
family.   4. Presidents—United States—Biography.   5. Washington (D.C.)—Social life and
customs—19th century.   6. White House (Washington, D.C.)—History—19th century.
7. Lincoln, Abraham, 1809–1865—Friends and associates.   8. Bayne, Julia Taft, 1845–1933—
Childhood and youth.   I. Title.
E457.15 .B36 2001
973.7′092—dc21
[B]   2001033591

To
My Children

Contents

Illustrations

MARY A. DECREDICO

Introduction

Abraham Lincoln remains one of this nation's most beloved and revered presidents. His elevation to iconic status came quickly after he was killed prematurely by John Wilkes Booth in April 1865. The man known variously as the Great Emancipator, the Savior of the Union, and Father Abraham did not live to see the end of the war that preserved the nation he held so dear.

It is—and has been—hard to separate the "real" Lincoln from the deified image most historians and biographers have crafted since his death in 1865. Essayist Edmund Wilson once wrote, "There has undoubtedly been written about him more romantic and sentimental rubbish than any other American figure, with the possible exception of Edgar Allen Poe."[1] Other scholars have noted that Lincoln will forever be separated from history by the circumstances of his assassination. Even Lincoln's most even-handed biographers, such as David Donald, have portrayed a man destined for greatness. How refreshing it is—and how different— to view Lincoln through the eyes of a bright, sophisticated sixteen-year-old girl. Julia Taft Bayne's *Tad Lincoln's Father* is a delightful, albeit sentimentalized, look at President and Mrs. Lincoln and their beloved sons, Willie and Tad, during the early years of Lincoln's presidency. The picture we see is of doting parents who refuse to let secession and a bloody civil war interfere with their sons' childhood.

Julia Taft Bayne was the vivacious daughter of Judge Horatio N.

1. Edmund Wilson, *Patriotic Gore: Studies in the Literature of the American Civil War* (New York: Oxford University Press, 1962), 115.

Taft, who had managed to have President James Buchanan appoint him chief of the U.S. Patent Office. Although Taft was a native New Yorker and had served the Empire State in a number of official positions, he quickly became friends with other members of the very pro-Southern Buchanan administration. Perhaps Taft was a doughface, a term used to describe Northerners who had strong Southern leanings and often pro-slavery sentiments. The Tafts did have two black servants, slaves who had been leased from their owner in Virginia, who, according to Julia, had nothing but disdain for the abolitionists. And Julia Taft makes mention of the numerous Southern senators who begged her father to cast his lot with the South once secession loomed on the horizon. Taft's position within the Patent Office and his friendship with Buchanan and other luminaries assured the family of a high profile within the nation's capital.

Julia relished her encounters with President Buchanan and his official hostess, Harriet Lane, his niece. She admitted they probably did not know her name, but her attendance at the prestigious Madame Smith's French School gave her a type of status other young girls may have lacked. Indeed, Julia Taft frequently darted through the White House grounds on her way to and from school. Often she had the good fortune to bump into the president and Miss Lane. They conversed with her in French and obviously saw nothing unusual about the fact young Julia used the White House as a shortcut to school and home. For Julia Taft, James Buchanan was the perfect gentleman every chief executive should be. Obviously she regretted the change in administrations when Abraham Lincoln became President on March 4, 1861.

Yet Julia Taft would quickly find herself again a guest of the president after Lincoln was inaugurated. Shortly after those festivities, Julia and her younger brothers, Horatio Nelson Jr., known as Bud, and Halsey Cook Taft, called Holly, were invited to the White House to play with Willie and Tad Lincoln. Mary Lincoln, who had met Julia's parents, knew that the Taft boys, at twelve and eight, were almost the same ages as her two sons. Having left their playmates behind in Springfield, Illinois, the young Lincoln boys were lonely for fun. Thus began the frequent visits of Bud, Holly, and Julia to the White House, visits that lasted until Willie's death in 1862.

Julia Taft Bayne's book, published more than sixty years after her initial meeting with Lincoln, does have elements of nostalgia and perhaps even embellishment. Still, the book is a charming depiction of Lincoln as father, an image often overlooked by scholars who focus on Lincoln as the war president. Julia herself makes no apologies for the picture she paints of the sixteenth president. As she says early in her work, "The Lincoln I knew and who lives in my memory with photographic distinctness has not the qualities of the Civil War President as presented in history." Those portrayals, as Julia acknowledges, are "heroic," if not saintly, and perpetuate the Lincoln legend. To Julia Taft, Abraham Lincoln was a tall, avuncular man who delighted in messing her curls, calling her "Jewly," and teasing her about being a "flibbertigibbet."

The Washington DC of 1861 was a decidedly rough and unfinished town that seemed to many observers Southern in tone and orientation. With a population of about sixty thousand, the nation's capital seemed, despite the increase in inhabitants, little different from the city John Adams moved to in 1797 when he became the first president to live in the White House. Locals decried the stench that hung like a thick pall over the city every summer. Located on the Potomac flats and situated near a sewage dump, the Executive Mansion was not immune from the smells nor the diseases—typhoid, smallpox, and malaria—that invaded the capital on a regular basis. European visitors found the White House a large, unremarkable building that seemed ill-suited to house the leader of the young republic. Americans, however, delighted in the open nature of the President's house. The doors were never locked, and visitors could be found wandering about at all hours, even in the first family's private quarters. It was the "people's house," and as Julia Taft demonstrates throughout the pages of her memoir, the average citizen availed himself of the opportunity to visit the president. It was not unusual for Lincoln to find himself besieged by office-seekers as he made his way to his bedroom, only to find more tourists admiring the curtains in his study. This marked lack of security may shock and perhaps amuse those of us familiar with twenty-first-century concerns. It would take repeated death threats to get the president even an armed guard on the front lawn.

Julia Taft hints at the great redecorating Mary Lincoln would undertake during Lincoln's first term. Determined to make her mark on

Washington society and the presidency, Mary Lincoln embarked upon an ambitious plan to refit and refurbish what had become a rather shabby residence. Frequent shopping sprees to New York helped her realize her goal. New carpets, rich wallpaper, and luxurious upholstery, not to mention new china and crystal, transformed the Executive Mansion into a beautiful showpiece, but at an exorbitantly high cost to the Lincolns and Congress. Visitors to the Lincolns' levees could not help but notice the changes Mary Lincoln's rich taste effected. Again attesting to the lack of security, many visitors, official and otherwise, left the White House with "souvenirs": pieces of drapery or carpet snipped while the first couple was either not present or observing.

Mary Lincoln's fondness for shopping also caught Julia's attention. On one occasion, Mrs. Lincoln discovered that the bonnet strings of Mrs. Taft's hat were the deep color of purple she desired. Mary Lincoln politely demanded to have them. Non-plussed, Mrs. Taft agreed, though she was less than pleased. To Julia, this demonstrated that Mary Lincoln always received what she wanted regardless of what others might want or think. This was the Mary Lincoln Washington matrons deplored as coarse and unladylike, more accustomed to the frontier than refined Washington society; this was the woman they gossiped about and pilloried at every chance.

That side of Mary Lincoln, the harsh, uncompromising woman who was disliked by the capital's elite ladies, appears only once in Taft's book. Instead, Julia Taft portrays a first lady decidedly different from the often shrewish matron Lincoln's biographers have described. Julia Taft states several times that she and Mary Lincoln formed a deep and affectionate friendship and that the president's wife allowed young Julia to speak up and have opinions that even Julia's mother would not allow. Julia notes, as have other scholars, that the Lincolns adored their sons but always wished to have a daughter. One gets the sense while reading of Julia's visits to the White House that she became for the Lincolns that missing daughter, or at the very least, a much loved niece.

To be sure, Abraham and Mary Lincoln were devoted parents. Relatives and visitors alike commented upon the wild and often unruly natures of Willie and Tad. Apparently, neither son was ever disciplined, a point that often enraged cabinet members, whose meetings were interrupted by Willie and Tad bursting into the room beating on drums. Many of the boys' antics tried Julia's patience, apparent where she notes editorially that young people were supposed to act thus and so, and the Lincoln boys never did. Readers gain a delightful look at a White House where children were put first: as Julia Taft notes, "If there was any motto or slogan of the White House during the early years of the Lincolns' occupancy it was this: 'Let the children have a good time.'" And they did. The Taft and Lincoln boys staged a circus and charged five cents admission; they built forts and played soldiers; they were often found frolicking with Tad's goats, Nako and Nannie, or with the dogs or pony that well-wishers gave them. Mischief often involved the president. As Julia recalls, she entered the study to find the four youngsters pinning down the president and begging her to help keep him down. On another occasion, Julia Taft recounts that Tad's doll, dressed in the gaudy uniform of a Zouave, was repeatedly executed for being asleep on watch. After the firing squad, he was accorded a military burial, much to the annoyance of the White House gardener, who found his flower beds dug up. Further misadventures in the garden were briefly averted when Tad garnered a pardon for the chronically negligent doll from his father. Julia Taft, while mortified that Tad would interrupt his father for such a silly request, benefited from the outcome: Tad gave her the pardon "papers" the president had signed. Such gaiety and high jinks must have helped to ease the increasingly heavy burdens Lincoln bore as the war continued and the pressures mounted.

The war that defined Lincoln's presidency appears at times in Julia Taft's book, but it never takes center stage. In a sense, it is strange she does not talk more about the war and the strain it placed on the president. We learn that after the firing on Fort Sumter, Washington was relatively undefended. Occasionally, Julia Taft mentions that her father and several of his friends believed Lincoln was destined for greatness, obviously more a reflection of the passage of time than of the reality in 1861. Lincoln's struggles with his cabinet, especially with Secretary of War Simon Cameron and later Treasury Secretary Salmon P. Chase, are not mentioned, nor is Lincoln's frustration with Gen. George B. McClellan and his failure to use the brilliant army he had created to attack the rebels. When the war does intrude into Julia Taft's memoir, her passages about it are simple and straightforward. She describes the arrival of the Sixth Massachusetts in Washington after its bloody visit to Baltimore, but again we notice she has a privileged vantage point to see it: she watches the review for the president from a window in the White House. Julia Taft also entertains the reader with accounts of her family and their socializing with members of the Seventh New York and of her visits to federal camps near the capital. Her reminiscences, while they speak of seeing wounded men, lack the drama and suffering other primary accounts convey. Perhaps Julia Taft, at sixteen, was unaware how horrific the war was becoming; maybe both her parents and the Lincolns tried to keep the devastating reality of things away from their young and certainly impressionable children. Regardless, the war, while it consumed Lincoln and his advisors, appears to have been kept as far from the young people as possible.

The Tafts' relationship with the Lincolns helped keep the Taft family in Washington and gainfully employed. After Judge Taft lost his job at the Patent Office, Lincoln intervened to get him placed in another position, so the family could remain in the capital. Throughout the period, Tad and Willie were frequent visitors at the Tafts' residence. Too, Bud and Holly would stay at the White House when Mary Lincoln was away on one of her many shopping excursions. The Lincoln boys also frequented the Tafts' Fourth Street Presbyterian Church (instead of New York Avenue Presbyterian, where the elder Lincolns worshipped), where all four boys attended Sunday school together. Finally, Tad and Willie and Bud and Holly were all tutored by the same teacher, usually at the White House. Thanks to the closeness of the family relationship, Julia had the opportunity to visit the White House whenever her brothers did. On several occasions that allowed her to meet many distinguished individuals, including the inventor of the USS *Monitor*, John Ericsson.

Some of Julia's accounts do not entirely agree with the historical record. For example, she relates that Lincoln visited General McClellan and took Bud and Willie with him. Bud told Julia that McClellan was out when they arrived, but they waited for his return. According to Bud, McClellan returned home, ignored the president and his young charges, and went to bed. Lincoln did visit McClellan on a fairly regular basis, if only to get the hesitant army commander to attack. But he usually took his secretary, John Hay, and the secretary of state, William H. Seward, not the irrepressible Bud and Willie. Julia Taft also relates that Lincoln appointed her as "assistant surgeon" to the Twenty-seventh New York regiment. Given the strictures against women serving even as nurses, especially young girls of sixteen, one wonders just what Julia did. She later remarks she served more as a secretary than a nurse and that the formidable Dorothea Dix, who chose Union nurses based on a strict policy, refused to consider Julia Taft for a position. Still, the arrival of wounded in ever-growing numbers found Julia pressed into service at her half brother's hospital, tending to the casualties. Here, one sees that Julia Taft's experiences were almost too real for the young girl. The blood and smells made her quite ill.

Perhaps the most poignant elements of Julia Taft's book relate to her descriptions of Abraham Lincoln. We are presented with a very human individual, always willing to chat and listen to the young people gathered about him. Initially Julia was shy of the tall president and acknowledged that she shrank from his kisses. But over time, a warm and loving relationship bloomed between Lincoln and the teenager. Julia is quick to point out how well-behaved and polite she was, and her comments on how her deportment varies from the time she penned her book (probably the late 1920s and early 1930s, when the book was initially published) again highlight a more genteel and formal time. But through her eyes, Lincoln is a husband and a father, devoted to his family and ever willing to make time for them.

Julia Taft also benefited from the Lincolns' library. A voracious reader who was forbidden to read novels at home, she found a refuge at the White House. Often while she read, she was joined by Lincoln, whom she describes as stretching his long frame on a chair in the study while he peruses the family Bible. Although not a terribly religious man, at least in the way of organized religion, the president was an avid reader and preferred Biblical stories. Over time, his close reading would be reflected in his speeches, most notably in those given at the Gettysburg cemetery dedication in November 1863 and at his second inaugural in March 1865.

Julia Taft's memoir also portrays a president and first lady who, while always available for their children, made a point of visiting and tending to the thousands of wounded Union soldiers that inundated the federal capital with distressing regularity. They would journey to hospitals, taking with them delicacies from the White House kitchen, to help ease the loneliness and pain of numerous federal soldiers. Mary Lincoln in particular liked to write notes to the young men's mothers to assure them of good care or of a proper burial. Such personal concern obviously touched Julia Taft and again underscored the humanity and goodness of the president and his wife.

The Taft children's idyllic life at the White House came to an abrupt end in February 1862. The capital, always prey to epidemics, was again ravaged by typhoid. During that winter, both Tad and Willie Lincoln became ill. According to Julia Taft, Willie called out for Bud, and the young Taft boy stayed at Willie's side throughout his long battle with the disease. Determined that a long-planned social event meant to alleviate some of Washington's gloom would take place, Mary and Abraham Lincoln spent the evening of February 5, 1862, alternately meeting guests and sitting with their seriously ill son. On February 20, Willie succumbed to typhoid fever. The president and his wife were grief-stricken. Mary Lincoln became almost incapacitated and grew so hysterical there were concerns for her sanity. As evidence of the depth of her mourning, Mary Lincoln asked that Bud and Holly Taft not attend the funeral, for they reminded her too much of the favorite son she had lost.

After Willie died, Julia, Bud, and Holly Taft were no longer invited to the White House. Apparently, their relationship with Willie Lincoln stirred up too many painful memories for Mrs. Lincoln. Soon the Taft children left Washington to attend school in the North. Julia Taft saw Mary Lincoln one more time, in 1864, at a White House reception. She was, according to her memory, warmly received, but that would be the last time Julia Taft would visit the Executive Mansion.

The Taft-Lincoln friendship experienced one last chapter. Julia Taft's half brother was a surgeon who happened to be in Ford's Theatre enjoying the play *Our American Cousin* the night Lincoln was assassinated. Once again, a Taft was close to the Lincolns during a trying, tragic time. Dr. Charles Taft accompanied the mortally wounded president to the house across the street, where he was taken after John Wilkes Booth shot him in the head. Dr. Taft stayed with the president all night and into the next morning of April 15, 1865, when Lincoln finally died. Julia Taft's father made a point of visiting Mary Lincoln before she left Washington. While paying his respects to the widow, Mary Lincoln gave him an ornate funeral badge sent from France as a memento. That badge, along with photographs Lincoln himself had given to Julia, remained treasures of the time the Taft children visited and played with the Lincoln boys.

Tad Lincoln's Father does not purport to be an accurate or scholarly account of the first two years the Lincolns spent in the White House. Julia Taft freely admits that her book is written from happy memories, with "no attempt at historical exactitude." Several of her vignettes do not ring true, and her portrait of her family's black servants smacks of the stereotypical jolly sambos. Her talk of being a crack shot, one honored by Berdan's sharpshooters, also seems a bit embellished with the benefit of hindsight. Nonetheless, there is no sense in the book that Julia Taft was trying to revise or re-make history. Instead, she reminisces about a delightful time in her young life when she was allowed the good fortune of being friends with the president and his family. Her recollections of egg rolling on the White House lawn on Easter Monday and of helping Mary Lincoln try on new frocks speak of a less complicated era when the Executive Mansion was always open and ordinary Americans could meet their president. It is noteworthy that the events she describes took place against the backdrop of the bloodiest war America ever fought. Julia Taft's book allows us to see one of the nation's most revered and admired presidents in a new light. We can see Abraham Lincoln in the place he loved most, his home, with the people dearest to him, his wife and young sons.

Foreword

To Abraham and Mary Todd Lincoln of Springfield, Illinois, beginning in 1843, were born with becoming regularity four sons, one about every two years. All of them were welcomed and loved, for both Mr. and Mrs. Lincoln were fond of children. The boys had their own way with their father; and while their mother was sometimes disposed to chide them for undue mischief, even she gave them quite as much liberty as was good for them. They were good boys, not prigs or saints, but good, average boys. When Eddie died in Springfield, and Willie died in Washington, both Mr. and Mrs. Lincoln were plunged into deep sorrow. Their greatest pride and hope was in their sons.

But with all this satisfaction went one sorrow. They had no daughter. We are not left in any doubt concerning their disappointment, for neither of them made any secret of the fact. Four noisy boys needed a sister, and both Mr. and Mrs. Lincoln were ready to pet and love a little girl.

The shyness which Lincoln felt in the presence of women left him when he met little girls. He admired them and liked them, and wished to have them about him. They were to him a happy reminder of what he had always wanted but never had possessed. And Mrs. Lincoln liked to have young girls about her. She was a bit conservative with regard to other women, but young girls were very dear to her.

That the Lincoln family at the threshold of their experience in Washington should have met Julia Taft, and invited her to come to the White House and play with the Lincoln boys, is something as pleasant to know about as it would have been natural to expect. In Springfield, the boys knew all the boys and girls of the town; in Washington, they were to make new friends under very different conditions. Mrs. Lincoln was solicitous in regard to the companions for her boys, and happy to have their friends at the White House. And so Julia Taft came thither.

It is very gratifying that Julia herself can tell us about her life as a playmate of the Lincoln boys, and at the same time tell us how a young girl saw Mr. Lincoln in his hours of freedom from the cares of office. Julia's narrative carries its own evidence of veracity, and it affords us a most interesting look into the White House in those grim days. Her story will find its fitting place with the permanently valuable documents of the Lincoln home, for it is a most readable tale, and gives us added reason for loving Abraham Lincoln.

The author wishes to make acknowledgment to the editors of *The Atlantic Monthly, St. Nicholas, The Dearborn Independent* and *The New York World* for permission to use in this book some material which originally appeared in their publications. Thanks are due Reed Taft Bayne for his assistance.

TAD LINCOLN'S FATHER

One bright windy day in March, 1861, my two brothers and I were sent to the White House to play with the Lincoln boys. At my mother's first meeting with Mrs. Lincoln it came out that my two brothers were about the ages of Willie and Tad Lincoln.

"Send them around to-morrow, please, Mrs. Taft," said Mrs. Lincoln. "Willie and Tad are so lonely and everything is so strange to them here in Washington."

I do not think either my brothers or I were much impressed by the idea of meeting the new President's children but we did not question the arrangement made by Mrs. Lincoln and my mother. In those days children did not question the plans made for them by their elders. I think, however, my mother felt that the occasion called for something a little extra in the way of clothes, for we were carefully dressed, much to the disgust of my brother, Bud, who could not see any reason for such formality and voiced his protest to Larney, our yellow girl.

"When white folks goes to see de President," said Larney, with the air of one delivering a social ukase, "dey has to dress in dere best or dey don't git in. An' it's de same when you go to see de President's chil'un."

We had been told to go to the front door of the White House and ask for Mrs. Lincoln, but instead of following instructions, we went in by the little gate near the Treasury. Assuring ourselves that things were outwardly unchanged under the new administration, we entered the office of Mr. Watt, the head gardener. Mr. Watt had his office in the building housing the conservatory, and during the Buchanan

administration we had come to know him well. Even then I had acquired a smattering of botanical lore and Mr. Watt delighted in showing
me over the conservatory and grounds and introducing me to strange
plants by their long Latinized names. I think perhaps he sometimes
made the names more complicated than they actually were for the fun
of hearing me try to pronounce them after him.

I told Mr. Watt that we had come by invitation of Mrs. Lincoln
to play with the Lincoln boys. My mother had instructed me to so
announce myself to the doorman at the White House and it seemed as
good a way as any of telling Mr. Watt why we had come.

"I think the boys are up in the conservatory," said Mr. Watt, and
he called up the stairs, "Here, Willie, Tad, here is somebody to play
with you."

There was no answer, but we went up into the conservatory and
there stood the boys by the water-lily tank, watching the goldfish. Such
nice, quiet, shy boys, I thought. In five minutes the four boys had
disappeared and I saw them no more that day. My brothers came home
at dark looking, as Larney said, like "dey done bin huntin' coons in
de bresh," but they had "had the best time; been all over the White
House; Mrs. Lincoln said we must come every day and bring Julia,
and Mr. Lincoln, I mean the President—she called him Mr. Lincoln,
anyway—jounced us on his lap and told us stories."

Early next morning Willie and Tad appeared, guided by one of the
gardeners, and spent the day exploring our house and the neighborhood, including the back alley where the servants lived. Our house
was the only one on the block with an attic, bathroom and cellar. It
was built by a Northern man and the cellar was an object of great
interest to children in the neighborhood, although of course the Lincoln
boys, being raised in Illinois, were accustomed to houses of this kind.
Washington houses did not have cellars usually and our neighbors said
if our father persisted in sticking to the Yankees, we might find the
cellar useful to hide in when the Southern army entered Washington.

Thus began an intimacy between the Lincoln boys and my brothers
which continued until Willie's death. My brother, Horatio Nelson
Taft, Jr.—never called anything but Bud—was twelve, a year older
than Willie Lincoln. Both were lighthaired, pleasant, rather quiet boys.

Thomas Lincoln—Tad—and my brother Halsey Cook Taft—Holly—
were eight. The resemblance of the two pairs of boys was often remarked. The Lincoln boys wore wool suits much like my brothers',
though our neighbors, who sympathized with the South, made fun of
the fit of their suits and remarked openly that the President's children
should be better dressed.

Willie Lincoln was the most lovable boy I ever knew, bright, sensible,
sweet-tempered and gentle-mannered. Tad had a quick fiery temper,
very affectionate when he chose, but implacable in his dislikes. A slight
impediment in his speech made it difficult for strangers to understand
him. They were two healthy, rollicking Western boys, never accustomed
to restraint, and the notice which their father's exalted station drew
upon them was very distasteful. Willie would complain, "I wish they
wouldn't stare at us so. Wasn't there ever a President who had children?"

A few days after this first visit I went with my brothers to the White
House and was kindly received by Mrs. Lincoln who placed me beside
her on the sofa. She was dressed in a fresh lilac organdy and looked
very attractive. She was so pleasant and kind to me that I felt at my ease
almost at once. From that day I was fond of Mrs. Lincoln and I have
a very sweet and tender memory of her. She asked me questions and
let me talk, which I was not usually allowed to do in the presence of
my elders. In the French-Washington, strictly chaperoned set, young
girls were not supposed to have opinions, certainly not to air them in
the presence of their elders. I came to confide in her in a way that I
would never have dared to do in my lady-mother. And I think, after
we became good friends, that she confided in me in a way that she
doubtless thought beneath the dignity of her station in conversing with
Washington ladies. On that first visit I was showing her my new hat
when the President came in.

"Well, who's this, Mary?" he said.

"This is Julia Taft, Bud's sister," Mrs. Lincoln answered.

"So this is Bud's sister," he said, looking down at me kindly from his
great height. I had jumped instantly to my feet, for like all Washington
children I had been taught to rise and remain standing when the
President entered the room. He came up and put his hands under my
elbows as I stood, and lifted me toward him, and I was afraid he was

Willie Lincoln
From the photograph given by him to Julia Taft, 1861

going to kiss me. He looked big and dark and very different from the men I was accustomed to see. Perhaps he realized I was a bit frightened, for he put me back beside Mrs. Lincoln with a few friendly pats.

After we were better acquainted, I was not afraid of his kisses. Whenever he met me he had a pleasant word for me, though it was seldom a long conversation. He would frequently pass through the family sitting room with a bunch of papers in his hand and he would pause to answer my "good morning" and pat my head or my shoulder.

Sometimes I wanted to ask him questions but I was shy and afraid of being laughed at, and I know I missed much I would be glad to remember.

He always called me Julie—not the French "Julie" but "Jewly." Often he called me a "flibbertigibbet." The first time he bestowed this pet name upon me I looked at him open-eyed, for I had never heard the word before, and asked him what that was.

"You don't know what a flibbertigibbet is?" he inquired gravely, but with a lurking twinkle in his eye. "Well, I am surprised, child; I thought everybody knew what a flibbertigibbet was."

"Well, I don't," I replied stoutly. "Is it a French word?" I attended Madame Smith's French school and was rather proud of my acquaintance with that polished language.

"No, Julie, it's not a French word. It's a good American word and I'm surprised you don't know what it means."

"I don't think you do, either," I replied, beginning to suspect that he was teasing me.

"Don't know what flibbertigibbet means?" he said, in mock amazement, but he was smiling now and I was sure he was teasing.

"Of course I know what it means and I'll tell you. It's a small, slim thing with curls and a white dress and a blue sash who flies instead of walking."

I do not know whether Mr. Lincoln invented this complicated and awe-inspiring word on the spur of the moment or had heard somebody else use it before. At any rate, I am sure the definition he gave described me rather well in those days, and was about the way I appeared to him, as he came to see me almost every day with the boys or Mrs. Lincoln in the White House.

TWO

The Lincoln I knew and who lives in my memory with photographic distinctness has not the qualities of the Civil War President as presented in history.

Mature study of his life has shown me that he was a heroic character, one of the great heroes of history. It is my lasting regret that my memory of him is not heroic. He was to me a good, uncle-like person, sometimes quizzical, but always smiling and kind to "little Julie."

I was sixteen years old the day he was inaugurated, March 4, 1861, and I first saw him in the parade on Pennsylvania Avenue that day. The evening before my father and mother had called on the President-elect and Mrs. Lincoln at Willard's Hotel. My mother reported that few Washington ladies were there. Incredible as it seems to this generation, the Lincolns were not welcome in the capital. Before the war Washington was really a Southern city. Such permanent residents as it had were mostly with the South, and Washington society for the most part took a similar attitude toward the issue of slavery. We were accustomed to the convenience of having Negro servants and a good many Northern people, like my parents, hired such servants from their masters, though they would have been horrified at the idea of actually owning slaves. The capital had buzzed for weeks with stories of the uncouth manners of the President-elect and his wife. Elegant Washington ladies raised holy hands of horror at the thought of such a rustic pair following the polished Buchanan and his accomplished niece, Miss Lane, in the

White House. So only a few of Washington's socially elect called on the Lincolns that evening at Willard's.

Late that night I was awakened by a curious jarring rumble. I ran into my mother's room. She and my father were standing at the window and below, on L Street, a muffled battery was passing. We were afterwards very familiar with the clink-clank of the caisson chains and the jingle-jangle of artillery accoutrements, but now all was wrapped in blankets and there was only that heavy jar. General Winfield Scott had the battery posted on the corner of 12th Street, and the next morning the artillerymen stood at the guns, the mufflings removed, ready to serve.

My father said to an officer of high rank, "General Scott has no doubt taken precautions"; and he answered, "He has taken every precaution, but God only knows what will happen."

They used to call General Scott "Old Fuss and Feathers" but he certainly served his country well in this troublous time, and when the inauguration was finally over and the new President safely escorted to the White House, the old general is reported to have heaved a sigh of relief and said, "Thank God, we now have a government."

My father objected to my mother's going to the Capitol. It was there that trouble really was expected. So we had chairs in a window of Clement Woodward's hardware store on Pennsylvania Avenue. Two or three ladies mother knew were there. As we took our places a file of green-coated sharpshooters went through up to the roof. The whisper went round that they had received orders to shoot at any one crowding toward the President's carriage.

Never before had Washington presented such an appearance on inauguration day. Troops lined the avenue and at every corner there was a mounted orderly. The usual applause was lacking as the President's carriage, surrounded by a close guard of cavalry, passed and an ugly murmur punctuated by some abusive remarks followed it down the avenue.

As the procession went by, I had my first view of Lincoln, sitting beside the outgoing president, James Buchanan. As I watched them I am afraid I suffered a pang of sorrow at the going of that lovable gentleman of the old school, President Buchanan. Up to that time he had been my ideal of what a President should be. On my way to and from Madame Smith's school I often took a short cut through the White House grounds. In those less formal days that was permitted, if you happened to be known to the gardeners. Sometimes, as I hurried through, I met President Buchanan or his niece, Miss Lane, out for a stroll and they would speak to me in French. I do not think either knew who I was, but the fact that I was a student at Madame Smith's school was a sufficient indication of my family's social standing in the Washington of that day.

Miss Lane was very beautiful, a blond with lovely blue eyes. She was trained in the English court and made a perfect mistress of the White House. One day she gave me a bunch of English violets she had in her hand and I thought they were her very own flowers, so delicate and fragrant.

So as the procession passed us on that memorable fourth of March, my sympathy was naturally more with the outgoing president than with the tall, ungainly man who sat quietly beside him, apparently unmoved by the unfriendly attitude of the crowd which lined the avenue. One of the ladies near us said, "There goes that Illinois ape, the cursed Abolitionist. But he will never come back alive."

There was a fixed opinion throughout the city that there would be an attempt to kill Lincoln that day. Cassius M. Clay had raised a corps in the departments to guard the President and the White House. He refused to allow my father to enlist. "You have yourself and family to look out for," he said. My father, Judge H. N. Taft, had been a New York Democrat when he was appointed Chief Examiner in the Patent Office by President Buchanan. He had been a member of the famous constitutional convention in New York and at one time judge of the lower courts, from which office, I suppose, he derived the title of judge, always used in connection with his name in Washington. As an office holder under a Democratic President he naturally made friends with many Southern Democrats, and the war meant for him and for all of us the tragic breaking of many warm friendships. When the question of secession from the Union came up, he declared himself a Union man. This, of course, alienated his Southern friends. Some of them had backed him for his appointment and felt that he should repay that help by going with the South. These Southerners would stamp up and down our parlor, pleading, cajoling and even threatening in their effort to get father to change his mind and go with the Confederacy. Perhaps the fact that he was the recognized authority in the Patent Office on steam and firearms made them feel that he would be valuable to the Southern cause. I remember Senator Yulee, of Florida, shaking his fist in my father's face and shouting, "I tell you, Taft, when the Southern army enters Washington, you will be hanging on one of these lamp-posts."

I went with my mother to the senate gallery to hear Jefferson Davis' farewell speech. Mrs. Crittenden, the wife of the senator, sat next to me and she told me about going to the Jackson ball after the battle of New Orleans. "I had a beautiful white lace dress," she said, "and a wreath of jasmine, and I danced every dance and fainted dead away and was carried out in the arms of two gentlemen."

A hush came over the senate as the senator from Mississippi, Jefferson Davis, rose to speak. Tall and imposing, and with voice quivering with emotion, he pleaded the cause of the South. When he reached that part of his speech in which he said, "I shall never stand in this place again," a shiver of impending calamity went over the audience. There was something prophetic in the stern, inflexible honesty of the man. I gave vent to a few sobs, but my mother sternly said, "Julia, compose yourself at once." She did not wish to appear to sympathize with the Confederate cause.

Senator Chestnut of Alabama and Senator Sumner of Massachusetts had encounters keen and glittering as rapier bouts. A rumor flew about that the House was in wild disorder. We went there and found the rumor fully justified. The members, a wild mob, were on their feet, shouting fierce invectives, shaking their fists, while the Speaker pounded the desk with his gavel in a vain attempt to restore order.

Suddenly the great doors were thrown open and the Sergeant at Arms appeared, bearing the Mace before him. This baton, fashioned like the Roman fasces, bound with silver rings and with a silver eagle on the top, is the concrete symbol of the authority of the Speaker, and behind him of the Republic. Instantly these turbulent congressmen slunk into their seats before it and there was calm. The calm, however, which precedes a storm.

We went home through Lafayette Square and met Mrs. Eaton. My mother stopped to chat with her. She gave me peppermints from her black reticule and I was secretly mortified, for even if I was small and slight for my age, with long curls, I was dignified with the weight of sixteen years, and was too old to be given peppermints by a peering, near-sighted old lady. Yet I knew the story of Mrs. Eaton,—of how, as Peggy O'Neal, the beautiful daughter of a Washington tavern-keeper, she caught the fancy of General Eaton, Jackson's Secretary of War, who married her and raised a dreadful rumpus in the cabinet.

It started, as such things often do, in a church fight. President Jackson and most of his cabinet were pewholders in the Second Presbyterian Church of Washington, which at that time stood where the New York Avenue Church now stands. That, of course, made it the official church in social circles. Social and official Washington was not at all inclined to receive a tavern-keeper's daughter, even if she had married the Secretary of War, and when it was noticed that the snubbed bride was regularly attending the church, many members threatened to withdraw unless Mrs. Eaton did. President Jackson supported her. The pastor, Doctor Campbell, called at the White House to rebuke the President. General Jackson called a cabinet meeting and asked the pastor to present his charges, which the cabinet decided were without foundation. President Jackson, Mrs. Eaton and a large number of the members withdrew their pewholdings and the pastor was left practically without a congregation. Then President Jackson declared "by the Great Eternal" his cabinet members' wives would receive "good little Peggy" or their husbands could resign. Some of them did resign and the President sent home his niece, Mrs. Donelson, and dismissed his private secretary. Then General Eaton was appointed minister to Spain, where Peggy became a great favorite.

The Lincoln family attended the New York Avenue Church and I once told them about Peggy O'Neal and they seemed quite interested in her. Mrs. Lincoln said, "Julia is always raking up some old story of Washington."

So in view of this historic background, I forgive the old lady the affront of the peppermints and thank her for them. She and my mother discussed the stirring events of the last few days.

"These are troublous times, Mrs. Taft. Troublous times," said Mrs. Eaton in parting. "We need a firm, determined leader, one who is not afraid to use armed force." And she looked up at what Tad Lincoln called the "tippy-toe" statue of General Jackson. There could be no question as to the kind of a leader she felt was needed.

Somehow these events group themselves in my memory as associated with Lincoln's inauguration. I know, as a matter of history and from a study of my father's diary, that Jefferson Davis delivered his speech in the latter part of January, and I am not quite sure of the date of that historic occasion when the Mace was carried through the House, the last time it has been necessary to display it in that chamber. But with no attempt at historical exactitude, I set these things down as they live in my memory, impressions of that tense, waiting period when the war-clouds gathered for the storm that was soon to shake the nation to its foundation.

THREE

The President and Mrs. Lincoln attended the New York Avenue Presbyterian Church, but it was not long before Willie and Tad formed the habit of going with us to the Fourth Presbyterian, of which Doctor J. C. Smith was pastor. Many in our church were in sympathy with the secessionists, and when Doctor Smith prayed for the President of the United States they would express their disapproval by rising and leaving the church, banging their pew doors and the outside door on their way out. This went on for several weeks until one Sunday a slim young lieutenant appeared with a file of soldiers. When the hour for service arrived the lieutenant marched to the front of the church, wheeled, and in a crisp, military tone, announced:

"It is the order of the Provost Marshal that any one disturbing this service or leaving it before it is out will be arrested and taken to the guardhouse."

It seemed to me that Doctor Smith prayed rather longer and more fervently than usual that day for the President but there was no disturbance on the part of secessionists. Tad Lincoln was frankly disappointed. The indignant exodus of the secessionists with their banging of pew doors had been a welcome respite in the long prayer. He had more than once remarked, "I don't see why preachers always pray so long for Pa." After the service he expressed his scorn of the "Secesshes," as he called them, for not accepting the lieutenant's challenge.

"If I was Secesh," said Tad, "I wouldn't let him stop me banging pew doors."

"Yes," answered Willie, "and get put in the guardhouse."

"Well, I guess Pa could get me out," was Tad's answer.

I remember that Sunday, as Tad sat on the floor of the pew, as he usually did amusing himself with whatever he had in his pocket, a young officer, who was with us, gave him his knife, thinking Tad could not open it. But he did and cut his finger and I had to bind it up with my best embroidered handkerchief. I hissed, "I will never take you to church again, Thomas Lincoln." Some biographers of Lincoln call Tad's name Thaddeus. That is a mistake. Other writers represent the boys as calling their parents "Papa-day" and "Mama-day." I never heard them call their father and mother by any other name than Pa (paw) and Ma (maw), with the broad accent. Tad hated to be called Thomas. It was his grandfather's name and I never called him by it except when I was angry.

Now he replied, to my horror, out loud, "Just you keep your eyes on Willie, sitting there good as pie."

It may have been the next day or perhaps a day or two later, while we were playing in the sitting room of the White House, that the President asked me:

"Why do our boys like to go to your church, Julie?" I have a distinct recollection of him as he put that question to me. He was sprawled out in his big chair by the window and there was a book upon his lap which he had been reading. It may have been his Bible. The big, worn leather-covered book stood on a small table ready to his hand and quite often, after the midday meal, he would sit there reading, sometimes in his stocking feet with one long leg crossed over the other, the unshod foot slowly waving back and forth, as if in time to some inaudible music. Mrs. Lincoln sometimes protested against this habit of sitting in his stocking feet and would order a servant to bring his slippers. Again, I have heard her criticize his cuffs for being a trifle more frayed than was becoming to his position, but I do not think these wifely admonitions made much impression upon Mr. Lincoln. Now he sat there, peering kindly at me over his glasses.

"Yes," said Mrs. Lincoln. "Why do Willie and Tad like your church? They won't go to Doctor Gurley's unless Bud and Holly go too."

"Why," I answered, "I reckon our church is livelier."

"Do you think it is livelier, Willie?" asked Mrs. Lincoln.

"Oh, yes," answered Willie. "Lots livelier. Only, maybe it won't be as lively any more." And he told of the coming of the provost guard and the effect of the lieutenant's threat upon the pew-door banging secessionists.

"And, Pa," demanded Tad, breaking in with his oft-voiced grievance, "why do the preachers always pray so long for you, Pa?"

"Well, Tad," said Mr. Lincoln, and I noticed he was no longer smiling but looked sad and worried. "I suppose it's because the preachers think I need it and," he continued softly, gazing away from us out of the window, "I guess I do."

"And, Pa," persisted Tad, unabashed by the gravity of his father's attitude, "Julie said, 'See the Lieutenant, how still he sits.' And I said, 'I bet he wouldn't sit so still if a bee stung him.' And she said, 'Yes, he would.' Do you think he would sit so still, Pa, if a bee was stinging him?"

"Yes," said the President. "I think he would, Tad." But he did not laugh with the rest of us and went off gravely to his office.

I have a very tender memory of Mrs. Lincoln, who was always so good to me. More than once she said, "I wish I had a little girl like you, Julia." She always called me Julia, although the boys, like their father, usually changed my name to Julie. I think both she and the President would have been glad to have a daughter. She told me about her little son Edward, who was between Robert and Willie, and who had died in infancy, and we wept together as she told me about his death. Once, a long time after this, I spoke of a boy friend who had joined the Confederate army and she said, "Yes, dear, it is sad when our friends are in the rebel army." I had heard that two brothers of Mrs. Lincoln were in that army and she may have been thinking of them when she comforted me but I never heard her actually speak of them. She said rebel army, not Southern or Confederate army but "rebel." Mrs. Lincoln was wickedly maligned by people saying that she was in sympathy with the South, but I am sure she was unreservedly for the Union and at one with her husband. I showed her an impassioned appeal from this boy friend to, "fly with me to the Southern clime before Washington is destroyed." I would not have dared to annoy my lady-mother with such trivial things, but the First Lady was not too exalted to sympathize with my story and give kind advice.

She would ask me to play my pieces of music to her. When I was asked to play, I had to play, no doubt of that. My parents had drilled into me the idea that it was an unforgivable breach of etiquette to refuse. I never practiced if I could help it and I would leave out a part of my "piece" if I could get by with it. If I heard talking behind me I went on fairly well, but if they actually listened, I nearly fell off the piano stool. When I played for Mrs. Lincoln, she would stand beside me to the last note, turning the leaves of my music. Somehow I never minded playing for her.

She gave me several pieces. One was "Colonel Ellsworth's Funeral March." Colonel Ellsworth came to Washington with the Lincolns. I came to know him well and admired him. The news of his death was a great shock to me as well as to the Lincoln family. In the little diary I kept, I note under date of May 19, 1861, "Heard a fine sermon at camp to-day by Albert Hale Smith. The soldiers sang 'I would not Live Alway' so heartily we could hardly hear the band. Col. Ellsworth escorted me home." The day before he went to Alexandria I went with my brother, Surgeon Taft, my three younger brothers and the Lincoln boys to the camp of Colonel Ellsworth's Fire Zouaves to see their gymnastic drill. He called them his monkeys and they surely possessed the agility of those animals. As he stood at the corner, waving his cap and calling, "Come again," he looked very bright and handsome. The next day Mrs. Lincoln told me of his tragic death at Alexandria. They had a large military funeral at the White House. Major Watt, the head gardener, asked me to put the wreath of white roses on his breast. It made me quite faint. I had never looked on one dead before.

Afterwards, during the service, I was horrified to see Tad Lincoln and my brother Holly perch themselves on the back of General Scott's chair. And when he rose, of course they fell back into the arms of some members of his staff. I felt an impulse to tell the President about our pleasant visit to Colonel Ellsworth the day before he was ordered to Alexandria but I was told that the President wept at the mention of Ellsworth and I was afraid it would make him grieve.

The Confederate flag which Ellsworth was pulling down at Alexandria when he was shot, and which was stained with his blood, was given to Mrs. Lincoln, but it was so tragic a reminder of the death of the gallant young soldier that she could not bear to have it around and put it away in a bureau drawer. There Tad presently found it, and on more than one occasion proudly displayed it in the White House grounds to the horrified amazement of loyal citizens.

At one time, when Washington was gay with flags in celebration of a victory, a much scandalized neighbor came to the door and asked my mother if she knew that a "rebel flag" was flying on the front of our house. It was, of course, the Ellsworth flag. My mother had sent Tad home with it twice before. Some time afterwards, when the President was reviewing some troops from the portico of the White House, Tad sneaked this flag out and waved it back of the President, who stood with a flag in his hands. The sight of a rebel flag on such an occasion caused some commotion, and when the President saw what was happening he pinioned his bad boy and the flag in his strong arms and handed them together to an orderly, who carried the offenders within.

Sousa, the elder, composed "Colonel Ellsworth's Funeral March" and dedicated it to Mrs. Lincoln. The music, I remember, had a picture of Ellsworth in his Zouave uniform on the title page and Mrs. Lincoln insisted that it was my duty to learn to play it. Although I admired Colonel Ellsworth greatly and sorrowed at his death, I could not feel that learning to play his funeral march was a part of my duty to the dead hero. But Mrs. Lincoln insisted and with some help from my teacher, my mother and Mrs. Lincoln, I finally mastered the composition and Mrs. Lincoln had me play it for the President, who was good enough to compliment me in his kindly way on its rendition.

Mrs. Lincoln was very particular in the matter of clothes. She dressed well, as befitted her position, and when she happened to see a fabric, or a ribbon or a certain style that pleased her fancy, she would make life miserable for her dressmaker or milliner until it was added to her wardrobe. I suppose, as the first lady of the land, she felt that she had a right to have what she wanted in the matter of dress and this amiable feminine weakness—if it was a weakness—was responsible for a little incident in which the bonnets of my mother and Mrs. Lincoln played an amusing part.

My mother was the daughter of Captain Jeremiah Halsey Cook of Sag Harbor, Long Island. As Miss Mary Malvina Cook she had spent

Mrs. Lincoln, Willie, and Tad
From a photograph in the collection of Frederick H. Meserre, New York

her winters in the gay society of Charleston, South Carolina. Florida had not then been discovered as a winter resort. I remember her showing me an old treasured "Keepsake" containing her picture with the title, "The Rose of Long Island." It would have been vastly indelicate in that day to print a lady's name. But as a girl she had been a noted beauty and as a woman she was still careful to dress the part.

My mother's bonnet—we call them hats now, but in the spring of 1861 they were bonnets—was, her friends all agreed, one of Willian's most ideal creations. Willian was the fashionable milliner on Pennsylvania Avenue, where everybody who was anybody went for bonnets, also dresses. They had not begun to be gowns, though they were always "robes" to Willian. This bonnet, a delicate straw, was lavishly trimmed with purple ribbon embroidered with small black figures. It had long strings which tied with a bow under the chin. On the next Wednesday after the bonnet was sent home, I accompanied my mother to the promenade concert on the White House grounds. The Marine Band played there every Wednesday afternoon and at the Capitol on Saturdays. The Saturday concerts at the Capitol were public affairs but the Wednesday concerts at the White House were more formal and all Washington society attended, attired in its most elegant raiment.

My mother, of course, wore the bonnet, together with a purple and white silk over a moderate crinoline, and lavender kid gloves. I was dressed in white Swiss, much beruffled, but without hoop skirt or crinoline, which was an abiding grievance with me. But my hat, a large "flat," with black lace hanging around the brim, trimmed with straw-colored ribbon, with small black roses and a large bunch of ripe wheat on the side, was very gratifying and almost compensated for the lack of crinoline. The band had been playing for some time and after we had walked about for a while, exchanging greetings with friends, the first notes of the national anthem brought those sitting to their feet, gentlemen removed their hats, and all stood at attention. Many people have the idea that this custom originated somewhat later, but it certainly was the custom in 1861, as I well remember. At the close of the concert my mother and I went up to the south front, where the presidential party was sitting, to pay our respects. I noticed Mrs. Lincoln looking intently at my mother's bonnet. After a few words of greeting, she took my mother aside and talked with her for a moment. While I could not hear their conversation, I knew someway that they were talking about my mother's bonnet and I was a bit puzzled at the look of amazement on my mother's face. I did not see why my mother should look so surprised at a passing compliment from Mrs. Lincoln.

It was nearly dinner time when we arrived home. My father was reading his *Star* in the back parlor. There were back parlors then, you know. Mother went up to him and said, "Horatio, Mrs. Lincoln made a most peculiar request of me to-day."

"What was it?" said my father.

She leaned forward and said something I could not hear, but as she stepped back and untied her bonnet strings I heard her say, "Willian trimmed her bonnet with this same ribbon but is unable to get enough for the strings."

"Well," said my father, "what will you do about it?"

"Why," answered my mother, "I suppose I'll have to let her have it and it's provoking, for I really did like this bonnet." Then she noticed I was listening and said, "Take your flat upstairs, Julia, and put it in the box." I went. We went when we were told in those days.

Next day we went to Willian's for the fitting of my first long dress. It had a train and was cut in the Victorian décolleté. I told Willian I was afraid it would fall off my shoulders but he said it was a perfect fit. I remember that the first time I wore it was at a presidential levee to which I was escorted by my father. After we had wormed our way through the dense crowd and the aide had spread my train within a few steps of the President, a great hulking cavalryman, just from camp with his spurs on, walked on my train.

It took some time to extricate him while I suffered agonies of mortification and my father was greatly annoyed. I saw smiles on some faces, but the President and Mrs. Lincoln never smiled or seemed to notice my embarrassment and they received me as though I were a "grown up" and a perfect stranger, which comforted me. Mrs. Lincoln afterwards said, "You carried it off well for a schoolgirl."

That day when the dress was being fitted I heard Willian say to my mother, "You is veree kind, Mrs. Taft. The Madame she want only that ribbon, not any other. If you give up ze strings, I retrim ze bonnet with lavender ribbon so it will be complete." So Willian sent for my mother's bonnet and in a few days it came back, more beautiful than at first, but now trimmed with lavender white-embroidered ribbon instead of purple.

There was a story by Miss Cleveland in the *American Magazine* some time ago of a Springfield merchant who had brought some patterns of organdy from the city and sent word to Mrs. Lincoln to select some before they were put on sale.

Mrs. Lincoln, accordingly, selected several but when she saw the one the merchant had chosen for his wife (they were neighbors) she wanted that one and threatened to return all the other patterns she had selected unless she could have it. And the merchant's wife had to give up her pattern and take another.

This illustrates the same trait as my story of the bonnet strings. It was an outstanding characteristic of Mary Todd Lincoln that she wanted what she wanted when she wanted it and no substitute! And as far as we know, she always had it, including a President of the United States.

Not long after this exchange of bonnet strings I reported to my mother, "Mrs. Lincoln wore a purple dress and those strings which were on your bonnet at first." My mother reproved me sharply.

"Never let me hear you make any remark about Mrs. Lincoln's clothes, Julia. The wife of the President should be above petty gossip."

But if an even exchange is no robbery, I am sure both Mrs. Lincoln and my mother were better satisfied after the transition worked by Willian. Mrs. Lincoln had the bonnet ribbons she wanted and my mother a more beautiful bonnet than at first. Willian had seen to that and at the same time lifted a load of worry from his artistic mind.

FOUR

Before the Lincolns came to Washington I had attended Madame Smith's exclusive French school at Number 223 G. Street. It was a big, dark house said to have been the quarters of the Russian Embassy years before. There was a dark stain on the floor of our schoolroom, which had once been the banqueting hall of the Embassy, and it was whispered that this stain had been caused by the blood of two Russian officers who had fought a duel on the spot for the favor of a beautiful Russian countess. I remember we did not like to sit over this stain but it added romance and delightful thrills to our existence in the old house.

It was said that one had to know who her great-great-grandfathers were to enter this school, but as I had a long line of eligible ancestors, the Halseys and Tafts and Cooks, not to mention Peregrine White on one side and the Earls of Taafe and Barons of Ballymote on the other, I was acceptable.

When my father and mother were making their farewell bows and compliments at the door on the day I entered the school, a young girl about my age dashed in from the hall and said, "When they ask you anything say, *'Qu'est ce, que c'est?'* Say it, 'Caska say.'" I said it. "That's right," she went on encouragingly; "say it to yourself so you won't forget it. It means, 'What is it?' If you can speak a little bit of French, they will be easier on you and you won't get black marks."

The Madame swept me into the schoolroom, introduced me with great ceremony, and gave me a seat. A teacher came and reeled off a few yards of French. I repeated my talisman. She smiled and said,

"Oui" several times, then led me to a class I afterwards knew as "first conversation." It was the rule that only French could be spoken by the pupils in the school. This applied to our conversation with each other in the gymnasium and between classes.

If Madame or the teachers overheard us using a word of English, a dreaded black mark was set down opposite our name in Madame's little black deportment book. It was difficult at first for one who knew only English and had to depend on a few faultily pronounced French words and the sign language to make oneself understood, but it was remarkable the short time it took me, under these adverse circumstances, to pick up the language.

Besides speaking French, we were taught deportment, to stand and sit properly in what was then regarded as a ladylike manner, to dance with a train and at the completion of the dance drop the train and give it a little backward kick out of the way and sweep gracefully to our seat. We were drilled in the court curtsy which, repeated over and over under the critical eye of Madame, was in itself a healthy form of calisthenics, as good as any modern form of setting-up exercises; we were taught the mysteries of the receiving line, precedence as necessary to the Washington hostess, and the proper forms of social correspondence. Of course, incidentally, we formed some acquaintance with the "three R's," history, literature and other studies, but these were not the important subjects in Madame Smith's curriculum. My father thought no young lady should come out in Washington society unless she could speak at least two languages beside her own, so he had me taught Spanish by a private tutor.

When the Prince of Wales, afterwards Edward VII, was in Washington on a visit to this country, he visited Madame Smith's school. It had an unusually fine gymnasium for those days and he asked to play a game of tenpins with the girls. I was one of three told off to play with him. He chattered gaily with us, speaking French fluently, and when I made a ten-strike he bowed to me with his hand on his heart. He was traveling incognito under the name of Lord Renfrew, so we were solemnly warned not to call him "Your Royal Highness" or to intimate in any way that we even guessed the dread secret that he was the heir to the British throne. We addressed him as "My Lord" and did our best to act as though he was merely Lord Renfrew and not the most important young man, socially and otherwise, in the world of our day.

Later came the grand ball given in his honor and *how* I wanted to go. I had visions of dancing with the prince and hearing more of that gallant young man's prettily turned French compliments. But my mother was inflexible. Tears and persuasions were of no avail. I was not "out" in society as yet, so I had to stay in and console myself with the enchanting memory of that game of ten-pins.

We three girls who played with the prince were given each a blooming rose in a pot. This was the only prize I ever received in school.

But if I was not out in society, I went to the opera and theater often. That was a part of my education. How the great names crowd upon me!—Adelina Patti, Susini, Brignoli, Parepa Rosa, Ole Bull, Murdock, Sothern in "Lord Dundreary," Booth in "Hamlet," Clara Morris, Mr. and Mrs. Drew, Joe Jefferson, Artemus Ward, Forrest in "King Lear," Gottschalk playing his "Last Hope."

I had begun, even then, to write verse and when the first Japanese embassy was received, my "Ode to the Japanese" was printed in the *Washington Star* and on being brought to the attention of the ambassadors so pleased them that they had their interpreter translate it into Japanese. The Japanese version was then beautifully painted on white satin and put into an exquisite lacquered box for presentation to the Emperor when the embassy returned to Japan. I don't know how the translator could turn the last lines of my poem into Japanese. It ended:

> Our Country's banner, broad and free,
> Shall be your guardian till you see
> Yourselves once more Japanned.

Madame Smith was horrified at that last line and insisted I must change it, but the editor of the *Star* thought it cute and printed it as I wrote it. I endured another outburst of remonstrance from Madame when she discovered that my poem was to be sent to the Emperor. What would the Emperor think of that last line, especially if he was informed that I was a pupil in her school, where she had done everything possible to inculcate a proper and cultivated attitude toward life? But the translator liked the idea of seeing himself "once more

Julia Taft at Sixteen
Washington, 1861

Japanned" too, so that was the way it went to the Emperor, much to Madame's disgust.

The arrival of the Japanese created quite a sensation in Washington. I went with my father to the navy yard to see them land. They had come on the frigate *Roanoke* from Japan with Commodore Perry and were transferred to the steamship *Philadelphia* at Hampton Roads. The embassy, with a large following of secretaries, artists and servants, was taken to Willard's Hotel. A day or two later they were presented to President Buchanan in the East Room of the White House.

Perhaps because I had written this "Ode to the Japanese" or perhaps simply because my father had influence enough to secure an invitation, I went with my mother to see the ambassadors formally presented to the President. Usually such ceremonies are confined to the President, Secretary of State and a few officials, but on this occasion the bars were let down and at least a hundred ladies and gentlemen were present. The ambassadors wore long trailing robes of gray, green and yellow, and each had two swords in his girdle which struck me as queer until I was informed that the high lords of Japan always carried two as a sign of their rank. They had what looked like little boxes on their heads and to us in Washington, accustomed to the showy military uniforms favored by foreign ambassadors on dress occasions, they presented a striking spectacle.

The Japanese bowed very low three times to President Buchanan, who stood with his cabinet members and a few senators and officers, waiting to receive them. Then, bowing again most ceremoniously, they presented to the President a red box containing the treaty. Then they retired into the Blue Room, returning a moment later with more elaborate bows and their credentials. Again they withdrew to enter with a succession of low bows and hand the President a letter from the Emperor.

I saw them all a few days later in my father's room in the Patent Office, where they had gone to see models of the early steam engines. They seemed very much interested in steam. A guard was stationed outside the door to keep out the crowd which insisted on trailing the Japanese about the city. My father had all the models brought from their eases and through an interpreter explained how they worked.

In the party was a Japanese boy a little younger than myself, with whom I became well acquainted. He had a long, complicated, high-sounding name that I never was able to pronounce, and to me and every one else in Washington at the time he was known as Japanese Tommy. He could speak a little English and I presented him with paper, envelopes, pens and pencil, which he put in his big sleeves and gave me in return a beautiful fan. While we were talking, a gentleman from the State Department took out his immaculate linen handkerchief, blew his nose vigorously and returned the handkerchief to his pocket.

Tommy was greatly horrified and seizing my arms, exclaimed, "Oh, no, no, no. Not do, not do!" Then he took a little package of squares of silky paper from his sleeve pocket, went through the motions of blowing his nose privately, and dropped the little square of paper in the wastebasket. He presented me with one of the packages of paper and explained in broken English the unseemly vulgarity of using a pocket handkerchief more than once. After this demonstration I certainly would not have blown my nose in the presence of a Japanese. And I daresay some modern doctors would agree that Tommy was right in his objection to handkerchiefs.

He wanted to present me to the ambassadors but I held back. He made a low bow and said, "You can do?"

"Oh, yes," I answered and swept the court curtsy we were taught at Madame's school. Tommy seemed delighted and led me to the Japanese princes; I curtsied in my best manner and they seemed pleased. One gave me a fan and the other a lovely scarf.

The ambassadors had brought to America a wonderful set of china, the pieces set with diamonds, pearls and rubies which, together with some rich gold-embroidered court vestments, were intended as presents from the Emperor to the President. But President Buchanan said, "The President of the United States does not receive presents," so the gifts were stored in the Treasury vaults.

In the fall of 1860 Madame Smith closed her school and went to Richmond. A Miss Douglas continued the school for a few weeks but conditions in Washington became so unsettled that the school was finally closed. Miss Mary Harlan, daughter of Senator Harlan of Iowa, attended the school and, I remember, played the harp divinely.

I had a great admiration for her though she said, "*Taisez-vous, taisez-vous,*" to me when I whispered. She married Robert Lincoln, President Lincoln's eldest son, who was away at school most of the year in which I was intimate with the Lincoln family. That fall I was placed by my father in Elmira College, where I was a puzzle to the faculty. I was speaking French and Spanish fluently and was conversant with French history and literature. I could enter the senior class in English literature and history and in botany and physiology, but I fell down into the lowest class in mathematics. But my time there was short, for when it appeared certain that Virginia would secede, perhaps taking the District of Columbia with her, my father telegraphed the president of Elmira to send me home at once. So they put me in charge of the sheriff of that county, who was going to the inauguration, and in his charge, feeling half like a convict on the way to the gallows, I returned home to my family in Washington.

Neither of my parents, I think, believed in slavery, but up to the time of the Emancipation Proclamation, both of our two servants were slaves, hired by the year from their master, who lived somewhere in Virginia. Aunt Kitty, our cook, was a fat, rather old Woman, very black, a devoted Methodist, given to fits of "the Power," when she would lie in the aisle of the Wesley Chapel and kick and yell and sing and be assisted home by two of the brethren, happy and exhausted, but able to proclaim joyously, "Bress de Lord, I done bin saved." Yet she had a practical belief in voodoo and was always on the lookout for "spells" and having her "footsteps picked up" by an enemy. She, in common with other Washington Negroes, had a fear of the Night Doctor, a ghastly being who was supposed to haunt the streets on dark and stormy nights. "If you see him you'll be right sick, but if he breeves in yer face you're done gone daid." My father was tall and often wore an ample long blue cloak which flapped in the wind and he said that sometimes, when he came home late on a stormy night, he saw Negroes crowd against a wall as he passed and cover their faces.

One day when Aunt Kitty was calling on the groom of Horace F. Clark, who lived on the next corner, she drank some horse liniment. "Why, Aunt Kitty," protested my mother, when she told her, "it might have killed you."

"No, mum, no, mum," replied Aunt Kitty, "it done cured me of a powerful fit of the conjur sickness. It sure did."

Early in April even the horde of office seekers fled northward and for several weeks Washington was left forlorn and defenseless. Rumor was that Lincoln had given orders to evacuate Fort Sumter and the wisdom of this course furnished the subject for heated arguments wherever people gathered. Some thought Virginia would join the Confederacy, others were as certain that she would remain in the Union. Then the city was electrified by the news that Sumter had been fired on and a few days later that the fort had fallen. Wild rumors spread that Norfolk and Harper's Ferry had been burned, that Virginia had left the Union and that Confederate gunboats were on the way up the river to shell Washington. There was one Sunday—I do not remember the date, but I know it was Sunday—when Washington at last realized that it was entirely cut off from the North. Wires were down and rails torn up, and the city shivered in fear of a mob of Baltimore "plug-uglies" that were reported on the way to burn and pillage.

Tad Lincoln, whom we saw at Sunday-school that day, informed us stoutly that he was not afraid of "plug-uglies" or anybody else. "You ought to see the fort we've got on the roof of our house," he said proudly. "Let 'em come. Willie and I are ready for 'em." My brothers and I inspected the "fort" a day or so later. It did not present a very formidable appearance, with a small log to represent a cannon and a few old condemned rifles, but the boys took a great deal of pride in it and laid private plans for the defense of the White House in case the city was attacked. All that year the roof of the White House was a favorite playground of the boys, representing alternately a fort or the deck of a man of war, according to their mood at the moment.

All Washington knew that the Seventh New York Regiment was on the way to the capital but no one knew exactly where it was, and even President Lincoln was reported to be anxious about their delay in arriving and to have said to his secretary, "Why don't they come? Why don't they come?"

We went to see the Capitol, which had taken on the appearance of an armed fort. About the entrance and between the pillars were barricades of iron plates, intended for the dome, held in place by barrels of sand and

Tad Lincoln
From the photograph given by him to Julia Taft, 1861

cement. All the statuary in the rotunda had been boxed and the pictures covered by rough boards, while the halls within were full of soldiers, drilling. These were several companies of Pennsylvania volunteers who had arrived in Washington before the rails were torn up.

Besides these, the city depended for protection on a few regulars and district militia. There was a company of cavalry quartered in Fort Lawson, William Wirt's old home just west of the War Department; a company of dragoons at Burch's stables, opposite the Willard; another and the West Point battery in a house near City Hall, and Magruder's battery and some infantry at the arsenal. But everybody knew these troops were sorely inadequate for defense against the attack which the city feared hourly.

While fear of an attack thus held the city in its grasp the Negroes cowered under the great war comet blazing in the sky. The Woodwards had an old slave named Oola, said to be a native African. She was tall and large of frame, with gray-black skin wrinkled yet drawn tight over forehead and cheek bones, and eyes whose sudden glance made us wince as though actually pricked, with tufts of white wool springing from her skull. The other servants were afraid of her evil eye and "conjur spells."

To have our fortunes told by her was a terrifying yet fascinating experience. "You see dat great fire sword, blazin' in de sky," she said. "Dat's a great war comin' and de handle's to'rd de Norf and de point to'rd de Souf and de Norf's gwine take dat sword and cut de Souf's heart out. But dat Linkum man, chilluns, if he takes de sword, he's gwine perish by it."

"Hooh, ya, ya," she said, as I held out my hand with a small silver piece in the palm, "you gwinter marry de church and you better quit foolishin' and git ready. Go way now, chilluns. I'm right tired with all dis gallumpshin in de heavings an' de yearth. Wish tu goodness I'd died hundred yeah ago in de good ole time, stead a-draggin' long inter dis yere black publican ministration. G'way, chilluns!"

Before her strange sibilant expletives and threatening gestures we fled, her young Miss foremost, saying, "If old Oola curses you in African, you'll shore be right sick directly."

We told the Lincoln boys about Oola's prophecy of war, carefully omitting, however, the dire prediction regarding their father. Tad was greatly impressed and carried the story, as tidings of import, to his father. Mrs. Lincoln laughed, but the President seemed strangely interested.

"What was that, Tad, that she said about the comet?" asked Mr. Lincoln.

"She said," answered Tad, gratified that at least one member of his family appreciated the gravity of the omen, "that the handle was toward the north and the point toward the south and that meant the North was going to take that sword and cut the South's heart out. Do you think that's what it means, Pa?"

"I hope not, Tad," answered his father gravely. "I hope it won't come to that." But I noticed him, a few evenings later, looking out of the window intently at the comet and I wondered if he was thinking of the old Negro woman's prophecy.

Oola proved herself a prophet in my case, also. Her prediction that I would "marry de church" came true in due time, although not in the way I thought she meant. I knew I had no "vocation" for a nun's life and it troubled me whenever I saw a group of good sisters in their long black robes, but as some years afterwards I married a Congregational minister and was a pastor's wife for over forty years in several New England churches, I think Oola's warning was justified.

Another who predicted war was M. Jordan, an old Frenchman who lived across the street from us. He had been one of Napoleon's Old Guard. He would tell us stories of his battles and of his great emperor. Every time he spoke the name of Napoleon he would click his heels together and pull off the blue cap that he wore. My mischievous brothers and the Lincoln boys would ask questions, the answers to which would bring in the name of Napoleon, and count afterwards how many times he pulled off his cap.

"I made him pull off his old cap nine times," Tad would brag after a visit.

"Yes, but you asked questions out of turn, Tad Lincoln, and that isn't fair," Willie would object. It was a regular game to them. I was glad M. Jordan never surmised the real reason the boys were so interested in his beloved emperor. He was a very kind old gentleman and gave us flowers and delicious little patés.

One day I told him my father said there would be a compromise and no war. The old soldier stood stern and straight under his blossoming pear tree. "No, petite," he said. *"La Guerre s'avance.* War is near. I feel it. Many of our dear ones will lie dead under the guns." He sniffed the air as he spoke and I ran home and told my father that Monsieur said war was coming; that he smelled it.

This was a most anxious time for President Lincoln and we could see him grow sad and silent under the strain. Remembering the threats that had been made against my father's life, the Provost Marshal sent six loaded muskets to our house and they were stacked in our bathroom till Tad Lincoln and my brother Holly succeeded in firing one out of the window. It nicked the corner of Mr. Bartle's house, next door, the bullet whistling over the head of their old mammy, who was washing some clothes in a tub. She looked up anxiously and said, "Pears like dose boys'll kill somebody's nigger yet." After that, father had the Provost Marshal take the muskets back.

Senator Dawes dined with us. He did not seem very hopeful of a compromise, while Mr. Bates, the Attorney General, was gay. He gave us candy and all the boys marbles. He seemed to have an inexhaustible stock of marbles, for I remember his giving the four boys a dozen marbles apiece several times, all of them finding their way into Tad's pocket before the week was out.

Senator Dawes, like my father, was greatly impressed by the appearance of the President. He spoke of the unkempt and neglected look of Lincoln when he first saw him but said, "There is something about the man, about the face, which is unfathomable." Both he and my father were of the opinion that Lincoln was the man sent by Divine Providence to serve the country in the dark hours before us. Senator Dawes said, "There is something in his face which I cannot understand. He is great. We can safely trust the Union cause to him." My father said after his first talk with Lincoln, "We have found a great man."

Easter Monday is the day of the egg-rolling in the White House grounds and the two Lincoln boys enjoyed it hugely. My two brothers, with a basket full of hardboiled and gaily colored eggs, were on hand early to meet Willie and Tad similarly equipped. At the rear of the White House is a sloping lawn with soft turf. The players stand on the top of the hill and watch their eggs in a race to the bottom. The one

"Bud" and "Holly" Taft, Playmates of the Lincoln Boys

which first arrives whole is the winner; the cracked or broken ones go to the victor, who eats them or at least is expected to. There are always plenty of little Negroes who can eat all the over-supply of broken eggs.

One boy had a colored china egg, but when discovered he and his egg were thrown out. Tad said next year he would have one made of cast iron.

So those anxious days passed while Washington lay defenseless, praying for the coming of the soldiers from the North. And every day came rumors that the rebels were gathering in force and that the city would be attacked.

FIVE

On April 19, the Sixth Massachusetts Regiment arrived, having fought their way through Baltimore, and how glad we were to see them! President Lincoln reviewed them from the portico of the White House. My brothers and I, with the Lincoln boys, watched the review from a White House window.

A few days later came the Seventh New York, the wonderful Seventh, and we felt almost safe.

We visited Camp Cameron and saw the elegant Seventh digging in the mud but happy. They served tea and presented me with one of their tin coffee cups with a flattering inscription scratched on it. Thousands of soldiers, they said reassuringly, would be here soon.

By early summer, Washington had become a great camp, with more regiments arriving daily. Everybody breathed easier and felt that the war was as good as won. It seemed to us nothing could withstand this mighty tide of armed men. Franklin Square, near our house, was filled with hastily constructed wooden barracks which were occupied, as soon as completed, by the Twelfth New York Militia.

My father, a New Yorker, took these boys to his heart at once. Our table was filled with members of this regiment whom he invited to breakfast and dinner and we always went over to the square for dress parade. When the two Rhode Island regiments with Governor Sprague arrived they were quartered in the Patent Office and my father gave up his large room to the governor and his staff, only reserving a corner for his desk and his assistant. I soon became well acquainted with "the little governor," as everybody called him.

Mrs. Lincoln often told me when I left her to go to the conservatory and have the bouquet man make me a nice bouquet for my mother. He would take a perfect flower, rose, cape jasmine or Camellia and with his assistant tying the short-stemmed flowers on to broom straws, build up a structure of the size and shape of a cabbage, with an edging of forget-me-nots or delicate ferns. This was then put into a stiff paper bouquet holder and was ready for presentation.

One day, when the bouquet man had made an unusually fine bouquet, Mrs. Lincoln suggested that I give it to Governor Sprague. I presume she had heard me speak of him and surmised that I admired him greatly. But as I was proudly bearing the bouquet to my father's room in the Patent Office, thinking on the way, of a proper speech to go with it, Miss Kate Chase appeared, sweeping along the hall escorted by two officers.

Miss Chase was a reigning society belle and, as the daughter of the Secretary of Treasury, very much in the swim.

"Where are you taking those flowers, child?" she asked.

"Mrs. Lincoln gave them to me to take to Governor Sprague," I answered.

"I will hand them to the governor with Mrs. Lincoln's compliments," said Miss Chase imperiously, taking the bouquet from me. She was very handsome, beautifully dressed, and accustomed to have what she wanted, and she took the bouquet from me before I could get up enough spunk to resist.

I went back to Mrs. Lincoln in wrath and tears. "Never mind, Julia," she said. "You shall have another just as pretty for the governor when Miss Chase isn't around." But Miss Chase was always around. In fact, she married him.

More regiments arrived. Washington was full of uniforms and our life was regulated and moved by the bugle and the drum. Reveille, breakfast, morning drill, sick call, officers' call, dinner, dress parade, supper, tattoo, lights out, taps.

Then the beloved Twelfth were ordered to another place in the defenses and the Twenty-seventh New York Volunteers came, raw and untrained. Two regular army drillmasters at once took charge of them.

This regiment was from our old home town in New York and soon many were coming over to our house when they could get leave. When I asked one young officer how he got leave so often, he said, "My captain used to be my father's coachman and he's good to me." The boys had a good deal of fun but they had to keep a sharp eye on the stern officers of the regular army who were responsible for turning them into real soldiers.

The Chaplain was a tall, severe man who objected to swearing. Sitting on our porch one day, he was greatly disturbed by some teamsters who were escorting a string of army wagons, each drawn by six mules. He said to my father, "I am going to speak to them," and he went down to the next corner and hailed the driver of the first team.

"My man," reproved the Chaplain. "Why do you swear so? It is very unpleasant to hear and it does no good."

"Why, Chaplain," answered the man apologetically, "them there mules won't stir a peg without cussin'. They've been brung up on it."

"Well," remonstrated the Chaplain, "cursing isn't necessary, and I'll show you it isn't."

The Chaplain walked over to the foremost mule who stood with forefeet firmly planted, braced back in a determined balk, while the other mules were plunging, fighting and kicking. The Chaplain patted the mule and apparently spoke some encouraging words to him and the mule suddenly lifted his forefeet and dashed forward, carrying his mate with him. Followed by the other wagons, they went swiftly down the avenue, the drivers looking back in admiring wonder at the Chaplain.

Some days after the Chaplain was dining with us and my father asked what he said to start that mule.

"Well, it may have been what I said," explained the Chaplain, "but the fact is, I stuck the point of my jackknife into him, but don't tell the teamsters. I've actually convinced them that swearing isn't necessary to start a mule."

"Little Mac," as we called General McClellan, was my hero until one day Bud came home and told us about going with President Lincoln and Willie to McClellan's house. The general had not returned and they sat in the parlor to wait for him. When he and his staff galloped up to the door and dismounted, Bud heard an orderly say, "The President is in the parlor waiting for you, General."

McClellan muttered something, then went into the house and up the stairs. They heard him pull off his boots and throw himself on the bed.

The President waited a while longer. Then he said, "Come, boys, let us go home." And they went.

After Bud told me of this insolence, I disliked General McClellan very much.

President Lincoln seemed utterly impervious to slights and even abuse of his high office. Washington was not friendly to him. His life was in danger from many conspiracies. Only one thing seemed important to him—the preservation of the Union.

The President seemed to take a great liking to Bud. On more than one occasion he used Bud as a messenger boy, sending him on errands, some of which seemed rather too important to be intrusted to one so young. When Bud would return home and tell us about errands, my father would express wonder that the President should select a twelve-year-old boy as a messenger in place of the orderlies and official messengers at his beck and call. Perhaps the President thought the boy might pass unnoticed amid that atmosphere of suspicion and intrigue, or perhaps it was just because he knew how Bud worshipped him and how proud he was to serve him.

One day, in going through Bud's clothes, I found a card with some penciled lines signed by Mr. Lincoln. I asked Bud about it and he told me the President had given him this card and told him to deliver it to Mr. Cameron, the Secretary of War.

"And, Bud," said the President, "give it to Cameron yourself and don't let anybody else see it."

Bud went to the War Department and after some difficulty in convincing Cameron's secretary that he had been sent by the President, was admitted. Cameron knew Bud as a playmate of the Lincoln children. He took the card, glanced at it hastily, and throwing it carelessly on the floor, said, "All right, Bud, I'll wait for them." Bud, remembering Mr. Lincoln's instructions, retrieved the card and put it in his pocket, where I found it. The card, which I still have, reads:

The Secretary of the Treasury
and the President will call on the
Secretary of War at 12:15, noon, today.

> A. Lincoln.

It was characteristic of Lincoln that in writing this note he should put the Secretary of the Treasury before himself. There was little of the pride of position in Mr. Lincoln.

My mother would say, "I wish President Lincoln would always remember that he is the President." She called it his "provoking humility." Colonel Lamar, the marshal, kept his eye on him to shoo him into his proper place, the first, which belongs to his rank. He opened a door for me once and held it, and I was horror-struck. I could not precede the President!

One day the President said to Bud, "Bud, could you go out and buy me a pair of rubbers?"

"Yes, sir," said Bud, willing to be of service to the man he adored. "What size, sir?"

The President looked at his feet with a doubtful smile.

"I guess you better get me the largest pair you can find, Bud," he said.

Bud thought these instructions hardly definite enough, so he and Willie went to the closet in the President's bedroom and found one of his old shoes—or boots, as we called them then. Armed with this, Bud sallied forth upon his shopping expedition. He exhibited his formidable shoe to the dismayed admiration of several storekeepers before he finally found a pair of rubbers that would fit it. He did not tell any one he was getting the rubbers for the President, but when he paid for them, the clerk said, "I think your father must have the largest feet in Washington."

SIX

Doctor Barnes, the surgeon of the Twenty-seventh New York, was an old friend of my father and well liked by all the family. As he saw I had a good deal of spare time, he said be would make me his "assistant surgeon." I was at first highly complimented by this imposing title and had visions of assisting him in complicated operations and being sent to stanch the wounds of handsome soldiers, but I soon found that my duties were more like those of a secretary. He was, I believe, supposed to have a qualified assistant surgeon under him, but that young doctor, for some reason or other, still remained in the North and did not join the regiment while it remained in Washington.

When I proudly announced my appointment to my friends at the White House, Mrs. Lincoln seemed pleased, and the President, rumpling my curls after a habit he had, said laughingly, "Well, well. Little Julie an assistant surgeon. When McClellan hears that, he'll advance on Richmond at once."

It was about this time that the administration was being severely criticized by Northern papers for delaying the advance against Richmond and I think Mr. Lincoln himself was rather tired of the excuses offered by the army leaders. I have spoken of his habit of ruffling my curls. He would put his hand on my head and rotate it rapidly, causing my curls to stand out in all directions. This seemed to please him better than it did me. It did, however, serve one good purpose. It gave me a ready excuse whenever my mother criticized the appearance of my hair. I could always say, "I can't help it when the President musses up my curls every time he sees me." My mother had no answer to that.

Surgeon Barnes had many letters of inquiry from friends and relatives about soldiers of the Twenty-seventh. Some were sick, two or three shot themselves with their own guns, being unused to firearms. Some did not trouble to write home. The surgeon would scribble a few words on the outside of these letters of inquiry and pass them over to me to make into pleasant letters of reply. When the Twenty-seventh was ordered over the Long Bridge into Virginia I was given the duty of visiting the members of the regiment who remained behind in different hospitals and reporting their condition to the surgeon twice a week.

Two of the soldiers I visited were very ill and only fit for a discharge and to be sent home, in the opinion of the hospital surgeon. Accordingly I filled out the discharge papers, which, however, needed the signatures of the colonel and regimental surgeon to make them official.

So my father and I applied at the Provost Marshal's office for a pass to visit the Twenty-seventh, encamped in front of Munson's Hill in Virginia. We knew Major Slipper but were sternly, if smilingly, made to take the "ironclad oath" before a pass was given us. The pass was limited to two days.

With some difficulty we secured a Negro to drive us to the camp. He had an ancient horse hitched to a more ancient, dilapidated buggy and regaled us all the way with hair-raising stories of the terrible soldiers. "I don't trus' no so'gers," he declared in parting, when we arrived at the camp. "Norf and Souf so'gers is all de same. None of 'em keer who gits killed." Having delivered this final warning, he drew whip over his ancient nag and disappeared swiftly in a cloud of dust.

We were joyfully received in camp. My father was quartered with the surgeon and a nice little tent was put up for me between the surgeon and the colonel.

There were two or three women in camp, wives of soldiers, and one captain's wife had "sneaked in" without a pass. About the middle of that first night I was awakened by the "long roll," usually the call to arms when the camp is attacked. It is a low, monotonous roll of the drums.

I shall never forget the strange, weird sound of that long roll. I rose and put on my dress, a blue flannel suit as much like a uniform as my mother would permit. When I tried to open my tent flap, I found it fastened on the outside. Finally getting it partly open and peering out, I saw a sentry pacing back and forth before my tent. I hailed him and said, "I want to get out, please."

He answered, "You are to stay inside. Colonel's orders, Miss."

I could pull the flap aside enough to see the men hastily forming in line in the company streets and hear the gruff orders of the sergeants. Then the bugles called, "Break Ranks," the men were dismissed and went back to their tents, and all was quiet.

My father told me next morning that two pickets had been shot and the outside sentries driven in and they thought there would be an attack on the camp. Anyway, I am glad I heard the long roll.

We enjoyed our visit so much that we overstayed our pass. However, Surgeon Barnes got leave to take us across the river, and when we went on to the chain bridge we met a detachment of a German regiment guarding it. None of them understood enough English to read our pass correctly, though they knew it was a pass and recognized the signature. So they allowed us to go on.

I had a great story to tell at the White House next day. While I was telling my adventures to Mrs. Lincoln and the boys, the President came in.

"What, Julie, you back," he said, with his quizzical smile. "I thought you and McClellan were in Richmond by this time."

It was during the month of May, as I remember it, that Mrs. Lincoln went to New York to buy some furnishings for the White House. She sent a note to my mother, asking that Bud and Holly be allowed to stay at the White House with Willie and Tad until she returned. My mother consented with some misgivings. While my brothers and the Lincoln boys were inseparable, they spent almost as much time at our home as at the White House and my mother could keep some check on them. I note an entry in my father's diary about this time which says, "The Lincoln boys have dined with us every day this week." Very likely Bud and Holly made a similar record at the White House the following week, although my mother often told them not to "make a nuisance of yourselves by always staying at meals." When the President and Mrs. Lincoln had distinguished visitors at dinner, the boys would sometimes have their dinner in another room and declared that to be "great fun."

On the wake of my mother's reply to Mrs. Lincoln's note, Tad and Willie arrived in a driving rain under a dilapidated umbrella Tad said they had borrowed from the cook. As the four boys departed, lugging a large satchel containing Bud's and Holly's clothes, Tad called back, "You bet we're going to have a good time."

The next day my cousin, Lieutenant Andrus, was brought to our house, from camp, sick, and Mother and I were busy taking care of him for some days. Secretary Welles told my father that Tad bombarded the room where they were holding a cabinet meeting with his toy cannon, and that President Lincoln left the meeting to go out to comfort Holly Taft, who had pinched his fingers with some contrivance.

My father was greatly disgusted with these tidings and stored up a lecture to be administered to Holly on the crime of disturbing cabinet meetings.

I was instructed to go and see that "those young rascals don't tear down the White House." I was followed at a respectful distance by Larney, bearing a package containing clean blouses for the boys. When I reached the White House, I noticed a smile on the faces of the sentry, doorkeeper, messengers and all the servants. I followed that peculiar smile upstairs and asked for the boys. "They are in the attic, Miss," answered a servant, with that same grin on his face.

I ascended to the attic and as I opened the door, Tad rushed at me, shouting, "Come quick, Julie. We're having a circus. I've got to be blacked up and Willie can't get his dress on and Bud's bonnet won't fit." They had two sheets pinned together for a curtain, behind which was a crowd of soldiers, sailors, gardeners and servants. Anybody, white or black, who had five cents, could go up the back stairs and see the show.

I took away from Tad the bottle of shoe blacking he was flourishing and made him up with some burnt cork. I told him burnt cork would do just as well and be easier to get off than shoe blacking. Willie was struggling with a lilac silk of his mother's. The gown had a long train and was cut in the expansive Victorian décolleté. I pinned it up so he could manage it, then straightened the bonnet, which Bud had stuck sideways firmly upon his head. He was wearing a white morning dress of Mrs. Lincoln's pinned around him in billowy folds.

"Boys," I said, highly scandalized at these proceedings, "does the President know about this?"

"Yep," said Tad. "Pa knows and he don't care, neither. He's coming up when those generals go away."

Willie handed me a bottle of "Bloom of Youth," saying, "Put some of this on Bud and me." I swabbed them both liberally with the beautifier. Tad was singing at the top of his voice, "Old Abe Lincoln came out of the wilderness."

"Tad, Tad," I remonstrated, "don't sing that. Suppose the President hears you."

"I don't care if he does," answered Tad. "Anyway, Pa won't care. I'm going to sing that song in the show." I don't think, however, that he did. At any rate, it wasn't listed on the "official program" gotten up by Willie.

I had had quite enough and, thoroughly disgusted, made my escape from the attic. On the stairs I met Major Hay, who was rushing up and seemed angry about something.

"Have those boys got the President's spectacles?" he asked.

"I think they have," I answered. I had just seen them on Tad's nose.

As I went out, Tad rushed after me. "Julie, come back! Make Holly go and get us some spectacles. We have got to have 'em in the show. Major Hay's taken Pa's away from us; that old gentleman who is visiting at your house has two pairs. Make Holly get one of 'em. One he wears under his hat and one pair he leaves round somewhere. Make Holly go get 'em."

Mr. Myrick interested Tad because he wore his tall hat in the house. In reply to Tad's question, he said he did it "to sweat his head."

"But why do you sweat your head?"

"To make my hair grow." He was perfectly bald, but this was satisfactory to Tad. But he thought no one needed two pairs of spectacles. I disregarded Tad's plea and went on. In the lower hall I met the President, who took my hand and said:

"Well, here is Julie come to the circus. Having a great time up there, eh?"

PROGRAME.

I. PART.

Hail Columbia . . . . Troupe
Star Spangled banner . . . . . Billy Sanders, Tad Lincoln
Dixie Land . . . . Joe Corkhead . . . Bud Taft
Home Sweet Home . . . . . . J. King . . . Willie Lincoln
. . . . C. Donelson . . . Holly Taft

II. PART.

Banjo Solo . . . . Billy Sanders & Joe Corkhead.
Champion Dance . . . . Billy Sanders.
Laughing & Crying . . . John Ghiselli Joe Corkhead.

STOCKS UP & STOCKS DOWN.
Joe Corkhead, Billy Sand & &

The
STEAM ARM.
" " " " " "

III. PART
TO
Conclude with

THE BLACK STATUE. . . . . Tad Lincoln

admission . . . . 16 Cents
J. King . . . . Proprietor.

Program of the "Circus" in the White House
Printed by Willie Lincoln

"Yes, sir," I said. "They are making a dreadful noise, and they have Mrs. Lincoln's things on and they look horrid."

He threw back his head and laughed heartily. It was almost the only time I ever saw Mr. Lincoln really laugh all over.

"Come, Julie," he said, "let's go up and see it. How much is it?"

"Five cents," I answered. "But, please, I don't want to go. They'll make me help them and I don't want to. It's horrid of them to wear Mrs. Lincoln's clothes." And eluding his hand I went on downstairs.

Later Bud told me he stayed through the show and seemed to enjoy the boys' jokes. I am glad to remember that hearty laugh of his.

SEVEN

If there was any motto or slogan of the White House during the early years of the Lincolns' occupancy it was this: "Let the children have a good time." Often I have heard Mrs. Lincoln say this with a smile, as her two sons and my two brothers rushed tumultuously through the room, talking loudly of some plan for their amusement.

And no less smiling and gracious was the tall, spare man, half of us called "Pa" and the rest of us (as we were taught at home) "Mist' Pres'dent," with no thought of its high import—this gently smiling father who played with us and told us stories when those whom Tad called "plaguey old generals" gave him a little leisure.

When the President came into the family sitting room and sat down to read, the boys would rush at him and demand a story. Tad perched precariously on the back of the big chair, Willie on one knee, Bud on the other, both leaning against him. Holly usually found a place on the arm of the chair, and often I would find myself swept into the group by the long arm which seemed to reach almost across the room.

I wish I could remember some of those stories. Usually they were melodramatic tales of hunters and settlers attacked by Indians. I have thought since that some of these tales may have been based on actual occurrences in the President's boyhood and I am sorry that my memory is so dim concerning them. I am afraid the boys enjoyed them more than I did. At the close of one favorite story of frontiersmen chased by the Indians, he would drawl impressively, "They galloped and they galloped, with the redskins close behind."

"But they got away, Pa, they got away," interrupted Tad.

"Oh, yes, they got away." Then suddenly rising to his full height, "Now I must get away."

Whenever I see St. Gaudens' statue of Lincoln, I think of these story hours and my memory supplies the four little wriggling figures, all gone now.

President Lincoln liked to play with the boys whenever he had a little time from his duties. Willie used to say mournfully, "Pa don't have time to play with us now." Once I heard a terrible racket in another room, and opening the door with the idea of bestowing some sisterly "don't" upon my young brothers, whose voices could be heard amid the din, beheld the President lying on the floor, with the four boys trying to hold him down. Willie and Bud had hold of his hands, Holly and Tad sprawled over his feet and legs, while the broad grin of Mr. Lincoln's face was evidence that he was enjoying himself hugely. As soon as the boys saw my face at the door, Tad called, "Julie, come quick and sit on his stomach." But this struck me too much like laying profane hands on the Lord's anointed, and I closed the door and went out.

You may infer from the part I played in some of these incidents that I was a conceited little prig. But I really don't think I was. I was dignified with the weight of sixteen years, remember, although the President always treated me as though I was about half that age, and many of the pranks of my young brothers and the Lincoln boys deeply shocked my sense of propriety.

I was not the only one thus impressed. I remember the towering rage displayed by Major Watt when Tad ate up all the strawberries being forced for a state dinner. Willie brought the news. His mother said, "Now what made you do that, Tad? Major Watt hoped to have them for the state dinner."

I went out to view the despoiled plants. Watt was fuming, threatening to go to the Madam.

"The Madam knows it," I said, "Willie told her," and as he seemed in a great rage, I added, "He is the Madam's son, remember."

"The Madam's wildcat," snarled the head gardener.

One day Tad broke a large mirror in the vestibule where the Marine Band used to play at receptions. Some one had given him a new ball which he threw up and caught in reckless disregard of his surroundings. In due time it landed against this mirror and a terrifying shattering of glass was the result. Tad kicked a piece of the mirror on the floor while the rest of us grouped around him in speechless horror.

"Well, it's broken," he said. "I don't b'lieve Pa'll care."

"It is not Pa's looking glass," objected Willie. "It belongs to the United States Government."

Tad seemed rather impressed by this view of the matter, especially as Holly added, "Aunt Kitty says that if you break a looking glass you'll have bad luck for seven years 'less you throw salt over your left shoulder and say the Lord's Prayer backward." Tad darted out and returned with a handful of salt with which he besprinkled the velvet carpet over his left shoulder.

"How do you begin? Amen first, I s'pose, n'ever n'ever—oh, I'll have to get Pa's Bible to do it." But before he could thus equip himself for his difficult task, word came from the stables that Nanko had escaped. Nanko was a goat that had been given the boys a few days before, and they were training him to draw a small wagon. Immediately the whole ménage was intent upon catching the goat, and it was finally corralled in a flower bed.

The boys had many pets given them—dogs, goats and ponies, both of the latter, their favorite pets, being burnt with the stables when they were consumed. Tad had another goat named Nannie, who was greatly attached to him. Once when Tad and his mother were out of the city, in Philadelphia I think, the President wrote to his wife that Nannie had been found in the middle of Tad's bed, chewing her cud. She undoubtedly thought she would find Tad there. A few days later she disappeared and was never seen again. The gardeners may have known something about it, as they complained of her many damaging visits to their flower beds.

Another omen of ill fortune which happened about this same time occurred during the raising of a new flag over the White House. The story was kept out of the newspapers at the time on account of its possible effect upon enlistments in the North.

I went with my mother to see this new flag raised by President Lincoln, the date, according to my diary, being June 29, 1861. Arriving at our destination, we went to the south portico to pay our respects to the "first lady" and were invited to join the group by Mrs. Lincoln.

There comes before my vision the brilliant group of generals and their aides, some members of the cabinet, the cluster of ladies in hoopskirts and blossoming bonnets, and in the center the tall spare form of the President, so little known and valued then.

When the moment came for the flag to be raised, the Marine Band began the national anthem and all arose, officers at salute, civilians uncovered. When the President pulled the cord, it stuck. He pulled harder, and suddenly the upper corner of the Union tore off and hung down. A gasp of surprise and horror at the sinister omen went around, but a young staff officer, with great presence of mind, stepped quickly to the group of ladies and extending his hand, hissed imploringly, "Pins! Pins!"

They were supplied at once. Women had more pins in their clothes in those days. Mother took two out of her lace collar and some out of her dress. Mrs. Lincoln and the other ladies did the same, and the officer swiftly and efficiently pinned the corner and the flag was raised.

The band had continued to play and the people on the grounds below, standing at attention, did not notice anything untoward except a slight delay in raising the flag. When we reached home and my father heard of the incident, he warned us not to mention the tearing of the stars out of the flag to any one.

"It will be suppressed," he said. "Some people are so superstitious. It might affect enlistments and we must have troops."

In my father's diary is this comment: "Flag raised on the White House. Gen. B. much disturbed by an unfortunate accident. I trust he will keep his discomposure to himself."

But what do you suppose Lincoln thought when he saw nine stars torn from the flag by his hand, who was its chief defender? I think he felt a sharper pang than any of us, but with his mystic nature there was a strange combination of hard common sense. I suppose he just forgot it.

N. P. Willis wrote some memorable words about this flag raising. I think he was ignorant of the sinister omen, although he noticed the strange delay. I quote his words:

There was quite an interval as the band played the Star Spangled Banner. All eyes were on the President's face, on which was a curious problem of expression. Lincoln, the westerner, measuring the chore to be done, wondering if the string would pull the flag up. Lincoln, the president and statesman, with abstract and serious eyes which seemed withdrawn into an inner sanctuary of thought, feeling the scene's far reach into the future. Separately, yet completely, the strange face told both stories.

But this "omen" was not as serious as it appeared, though it was not until 1912 that Congress fixed the place of the stars representing the States upon the blue union in the order of their admittance. There were nine stars torn out, the young officer said. These probably represented Delaware, Pennsylvania, New Jersey, Georgia, Connecticut, Massachusetts, New Hampshire, Virginia and New York. Only two of these were torn out by secession.

EIGHT

The sixteenth of July was the grand advance "on to Richmond," and all day, to the music of many bands, the regiments marched through the streets and over the long bridge into Virginia. There were German regiments, not the goose-stepping type made famous by the World War, but of the great Frederick's tradition, and they sang the lively "Ach, du lieber Augustin" and Luther's grand old hymn, "Ein Feste Burg."

There was the Sixty-ninth New York, of Irish-born who bore the green flag of Erin with the Stars and Stripes, and the Seventy-ninth New York, the Highlanders with their kilts and bagpipes. Then came New York's French regiment, the Fifty-fifth, and as they swung along they sang that song not loved by czars and emperors, for when its wild minors whip the air, thrones fall and kingdoms pass away.

> *Aux armes, citoyens!*
> *Forimez vos bataillons!*
> *Marchons, marchons! qu'un sang impur*
> *Abreuve nos sillons.*

Other regiments chanted "John Brown's Body."

So they passed, elate, triumphant, with flags flying and guns wreathed in flowers. They came back, most of them, the morning after that Sunday when Washington listened to the guns of Bull Run. Willie and Tad were at our house when we returned from church, Holly and our littlest brother, Willie Taft, clutching their pennies and shocked that "they dismissed Sunday-school without taking up the collection."

Willie Lincoln, much excited, said, "Pa says there's a battle in Virginia; that's big cannons going off that sounds like slamming doors."

It was a disorganized mob that entered the city next day in the drizzling rain. Many of the New York boys knew where Judge Taft lived and remembered his visits to their camp, and they came to our house until it was filled to overflowing. My father was at his office, my mother had gone somewhere with Miss Dorothea Dix, and we children were alone with the servants. Larney, our parlor maid, said, "I always done spec Yankee so'gers got horns, but dese yere ain't got nary horns." Yet she took refuge in the coat closet under the stairs and howled for the Lord to save us.

Old Aunt Kitty said, "You chilluns don't want to let on that old marse favors de Yankees, 'cause dem turrible Lou'sana Tigers'll be here right quick and you'all better go hide in de gyardin." But we did not want to hide and when mother returned she gathered up everything eatable in the house, and that she could borrow from the neighbors and fed those hungry soldiers. A few years ago I met two old soldiers who remembered being fed at mother's hasty lunch. And when I was telling these stories to the Confederate veterans at their State home at Beauvoir, Mississippi, I saw a smile go round at the mention of the "turrible Lou'sana Tigers," and asked how many of them had belonged to that regiment. Two kindly and amiable-looking old gentlemen arose. I am sure that even in their younger days they would have been a great disappointment to Aunt Kitty.

I think both Aunt Kitty and Larney were secretly disappointed because my father had not gone with the South. Both had a great disdain for what they called "Yankee notions." When Uncle Newell and Aunt Jane from the North were visiting us, Aunt Jane missed her coral breastpin, which was found among Larney's possessions. When my mother expressed her chagrin and surprise, Larney said, "You know I wouldn't take anything from you or young Miss, but that bobolitioner woman ain't no quality no-how, so I jest natcha'ly gits car'less." My parents had been somewhat annoyed at my uncle and aunt's open expression of sympathy for our "down-trodden slaves," but these seeds of abolition were blown away by Larney's attitude and Aunt Kitty's scornful sniffs.

Aunt Kitty used to say to me, "Nigger folks has a heap of notions white folks don't know 'bout and dey oughten t' neither. I could tell yer heaps o' things but it would only skeer ye. But dares some things a body oughter know. When you go ter bed, put yore shoes wid de toes pintin' way from de bed, so you won't have nightmare, and cut off an inch of your hair at de new moon, so it'll grow."

The day before the proclamation freeing the slaves went into effect, both of our servants were hastily gathered up by their owner and taken to Virginia. Both seemed sorry to part with us but otherwise willing enough to go South, and Aunt Kitty in parting scornfully pronounced freeing the slaves as "bobolition foolishment."

That same day Sallie Woodward, who was engaged to my elder brother Charles, came in great distress, bringing her maid. She said her father was going to send his slaves into Virginia and perhaps sell them down South and she could not live without Sarah, who had been born on the same day as herself. Sallie had never buttoned her own shoes or combed her hair, and Sarah declared, weeping, that she "done couldn't live 'way from Miss Sallie." My mother said, "There are two vacant rooms in the attic, Sallie. I don't know what is in them." Where Sarah spent that night, no one knew, but she was free next day, although she was always, "Miss Sallie's girl" to everybody.

I do not remember ever hearing President Lincoln tell a story of the type for which he was famous, but I unwittingly furnished him one story which I afterwards learned he used in his characteristic way to illustrate a point he was trying to make. I had been telling Mrs. Lincoln and the boys about having gone to Arlington on a Sunday-school picnic before the war, and how General Lee—he had the rank of colonel then—met the bus and jumped us all out of it, and what a pleasant, gracious host he had been to us that day. We had one very fat girl in the party who was sensitive about her weight and had defeated all conversational attempts of the curious to ascertain it. She sat in the very end of the bus and as soon as all the rest of us were out, the boys drove hurriedly to the hay scales by the Negro quarters and weighed the bus with Lucy in it. Then, after helping her out with profuse apologies, they weighed the empty bus. And Lucy's weight was a mystery no longer.

Mr. Lincoln sat at the window reading a newspaper while I was telling this story, and I did not know at the time he was listening. But a day or two later Willie said, "I heard Pa tell your story about the fat girl to-day."

Naturally I was interested and asked how the President came to tell my story. "Why," answered Willie, "he was talking to some men about the war and one of them said he wished they knew how big an army the rebels had in Virginia, and Pa said why didn't they find out, and the man said they'd tried to, and then Pa told your story about weighing the fat girl."

The Lincoln boys enjoyed being at our house. Their semi-public life in the White House, with its servants, messengers, guards and secret service men, often interfered with their play. At one time they were busily engaged in digging a "rifle pit" in the foot of our garden over which poor Aunt Kitty wabbled with difficulty whenever she went for parsley or mint.

At one time they took a vacant room in our attic for an "old Capitol Prison" and shut up my little black cat and the neighbor's dog as prisoners of war. The cat spent the time on a shelf, while the dog rushed about with yelps and barks until their protestations became so loud that my mother ordered their release.

From our grapevine they would take the "praying mantis," an insect somewhat resembling a grasshopper, so called from the way in which it bends its legs and bows its bead in a devout attitude. They seemed quiet and peaceable, but when the boys rubbed their noses together, they would fight ferociously, tearing off each other's legs and heads until both were killed. The soldiers would bet on these combats, though there was seldom a victor surviving.

The boys made great exertions to raise a "soldier company" which they called "Mrs. Lincoln's Zouaves." They gathered up all the boys they could get to enlist. Only a few had uniforms. Willie was colonel, Bud major, Holly captain, while Tad wanted only to be drum major. They were promised light, condemned rifles, but I do not remember whether they ever were thus equipped.

They were reviewed with great ceremony by the President and Mrs. Lincoln who gave them a flag, but the company dwindled until, like the one Artemus Ward told about, it was all officers.

My father sometimes took the boys with him when he went out to the camps. He always carried a basket of apples, oranges, or what the soldier boys seemed to prefer,—large white onions. Soldiers then did not have a balanced ration, but lived on salt horse (beef), hardtack and coffee. The boys enjoyed these excursions except that Willie and Tad disliked the notice they acquired as sons of the President.

Tad had a terrible longing for what he called "a real revolver," by which he meant, of course, one that would shoot. One morning, after I had finished my revolver practice, Tad and Willie followed me to my room and Tad begged to see my revolver. As it was not loaded, I let him have it. He aimed it at Bud and pulled the trigger. I disarmed him promptly with some stern admonitions on the danger of pointing a revolver at any one, loaded or unloaded.

"You're not fit to have a revolver, Tad Lincoln," I said, "and I ought to tell your mother about pointing that pistol at Bud."

"Don't tell Ma," said Tad imploringly. "I think maybe she'll get me a real revolver and I give you my after-David I'll never point it at anybody." Tad was fond of offering his after-David (affidavit) in making an assertion.

My brother, Surgeon Taft, had an idea that girls should be taught the use of firearms in war time, and he superintended my rifle and revolver practice every day. I was called a good shot; indeed, once after I had told my Lincoln stories to a large audience, an old veteran came up to me and said, "I remember you well. I belonged to the Berdan Sharpshooters and you came out to our camp once with a party from Washington. We were doing some fancy shooting for the visitors. The colonel handed you a rifle and you slipped off your little coat and did some fine shooting for us. Do you remember?" I did. I also remembered the thrill it gave me when the colonel pinned on my jacket the regimental badge with its crossed rifles surmounted by a B.

Tad kept nagging his parents until they finally gave him his "real revolver." Among Lincoln's letters is one to his wife while she and Tad happened to be out of the city, in which he wrote, "Think you had better put Tad's pistol away. I had an ugly dream about him." I think it strange that his parents ever trusted him with a real pistol.

Tad had a handsome Zouave doll sent him from the Sanitary Commission fair in New York. But the only use the boys had for the doll, who was called Jack, was to hold a court-martial over him, find him guilty of sleeping on post or desertion and sentence him to be "shot at sunrise," which was done immediately, Tad and his cannon being the firing squad. When a grave was dug among the new roses and Jack was buried with full military honors. I told them condemned soldiers were not buried with honors, but they wanted the whole performance.

I was in Mrs. Lincoln's room as she was trying on a new dress, when a dreadful noise floated up through the open window. "What is that noise, Julia?" asked Mrs. Lincoln.

"It is probably the 'dead march,'" I answered. "I suppose the boys are burying Jack again."

"O Julia," cried Mrs. Lincoln. "Go quick and tell them they must not dig holes among the roses. Major Watt says they will kill his young plants."

I went, although I knew they had been told about this several times before. When I reached them, I found the "dead march" being performed with much noisy desolation. They had an old broken fiddle, a banged-up horn, paper over a comb and Tad's drum. It was enough to make any decent corpse rejoice at the prospect of the grave. At that moment Major Watt arrived and looked at the yawning grave amid his rose bushes in helpless anger.

He made a sort of hopeless gesture and said, "Boys, why don't you get Jack pardoned?"

The suggestion struck the boys with instant favor. "Come on, Bud," said Tad with enthusiasm. "We'll get Pa to fix up a pardon."

"Don't you dare bother the President," I objected severely.

"Oh, Pa won't care," said Tad, and accompanied by the three boys he clattered up the stairs to the President's private office. I followed, hoping to head them off, and found them arguing with Major Hay outside the President's office. He was objecting to their bothering the President and I was beginning to hope that he would get rid of them, when the door opened and Mr. Lincoln appeared.

"Well, boys," smiling on the group. "What's the matter?"

"Oh, Pa," said Tad, making a flank movement around Major Hay and throwing himself at his father, "we want a pardon for Doll Jack, and Julie and Major Hay said we mustn't bother you, but I knew you'd fix it up. Won't you, Pa?"

"Pardon for Jack, eh," said the President, smiling, but with a pretense of mock gravity. "You know, Tad, it's not usual to grant pardons without some sort of hearing. You come in here and tell me why you think Jack should have a pardon."

Major Hay, with a disgusted snort, stepped aside and we trooped after the President into his office. He sat down in his big chair, crossed one long leg over the other and put the tips of his fingers together in a judicial manner.

"State your case, Tad," he said gravely.

"Well, you see, Pa," said Tad, "most every day we try Jack for being a spy or a deserter or something and then we shoot him and bury him, and Julie says it spoils his clothes, and Major Watt says it digs up his flowers, and so we thought we'd get you to fix us up a pardon."

The President considered this argument with due gravity; then he said, with a twinkle in his eye, "Yes, Tad, I think you've made a case. It's a good law that no man shall twice be put in jeopardy of his life for the same offence and you've already shot and buried Jack a dozen times. I guess he's entitled to a pardon." Turning round to his desk, he wrote something on a sheet of paper and handed it to Tad, saying, "There's your pardon, Tad. And I only wish, Hay," he said to his secretary, with a sort of sigh, "they were all that easy."

Major Hay did not answer. He bundled us out of the door with little ceremony, feeling, I presume, as disgusted as he looked at the farce he had just witnessed. But I think the President enjoyed it as a let-down from his serious duties.

When we got downstairs, Tad exhibited the pardon with great elation, saying, "I told you he wouldn't care, Julie." On his official note paper Mr. Lincoln had written:

> The Doll Jack is pardoned
> by order of the President.
>   A. Lincoln.

Tad asked me to keep this remarkable document, saying in his peculiar speech, which I have made no effort elsewhere to reproduce, "Here, Julie, keep this; no more bury'ins in the grownd."

In less than a week, however, Jack was hanging with a cord around his neck from a tree in the rear of our garden. Tad said he was proven to be a spy. The last time I saw poor Jack he reposed on top of the cornice of one of the East Room windows, where he had been tossed by one of the boys.

But doubtless Mr. Lincoln felt that this was one pardon that could not be criticized.

NINE

During the early days of the war there were constant rumors of spies in the capital. Following Bull Run the rumors became more pronounced. It was whispered that Confederate spies had obtained the exact plan of the battle and just when and where the attack was to be made, and in this way Beauregard was enabled to concentrate his widely scattered forces in time to meet McDowell at Manassas. Following the battle, wild rumor sped from mouth to mouth that the city was full of spies, that a plot had been discovered to cut the telegraph wires connecting various military positions with the War Department, to spike the guns in Fort Corcoran, Fort Ellsworth and other important points and to take General McClellan and several others prisoners.

To our house came one day a bland gentleman with distinguished black whiskers to make inquiries about Mrs. Rose Greenhow. Mrs. Greenhow and her little daughter Rose often came to our house and we liked them both. Mrs. Greenhow was a dashing, beautiful woman and I admired her. She was a brilliant conversationalist, dressed in the mode and was a leader in Washington society. In the days before Lincoln, President Buchanan and Miss Lane had dined at her house, and even at this time she numbered many distinguished people among her friends, although everybody knew her real sympathies were with the South.

The inquiring gentleman, whose name I do not remember, but whom we afterwards heard was a secret service man under Allan Pinkerton, asked us a lot of questions regarding Mrs. Greenhow. Yes, she did seem glad to meet officers who visited our house. Yes, she had asked Bud and Holly and me about our visits to the White House and what Mr. Lincoln said. My father remembered that she had asked him questions about the regiments that had arrived. But why did the gentleman ask these questions? What was wrong about Mrs. Greenhow? He took my father aside and conversed with him in whispers and my father said, "Very well, I will caution the children to say nothing."

We were cautioned accordingly. We must say nothing about the gentleman's visit or his questions. We obeyed but we wondered greatly. Then at last the mystery was solved. Tad and Willie arrived one day with the sensational news that Mrs. Greenhow had been arrested as a dangerous spy.

"They've got her shut up in her house with a lot of other spies," said Tad excitedly, "and there's a guard at the door and they'll probably shoot her at sunrise to-morrow. Get your hat, Bud, and we'll go over."

My mother at first forbade my brothers to go near Mrs. Greenhow's house but after much pleading by Tad consented to let them go on condition that sister Julia should accompany them to see that they did nothing improper.

Accordingly we set out for Mrs. Greenhow's. We recalled the black-whiskered detective and wondered whether any of the information Mrs. Greenhow had gleaned from us had been sent to Richmond. It made us, especially Bud and Holly, feel most important. Tad had never met her but regaled us with the false information he would have given had she tried her wiles on him. Mrs. Greenhow lived in a quiet, unpretentious house at Number 398 Sixteenth Street. We found a crowd of curiosity seekers in front and a detachment of Sturgis Rifles, General McClellan's bodyguard, surrounding the house. We knew the young lieutenant in charge, but he was on duty and refused to talk.

We found out afterwards that Mrs. Greenhow had been arrested secretly several days before the news leaked out and that several of her spies had visited her house and fallen into the detectives' trap. It was little Rose who at last gave the alarm and perhaps prevented the capture of other Confederate agents. The detectives kept constant watch on Mrs. Greenhow and her servants, including Lizzie Fitzgerald, a quick-witted Irish maid. But little Rose was allowed to go out into the garden to play. Climbing a tree she hung over the garden wall, calling to passers-by, "Mother has been arrested. Mother has been arrested," until Pinkerton's men at last heard her and carried her indoors. But enough people had heard little Rose to make it impossible to keep Mrs. Greenhow's arrest secret any longer.

Once arrested, Mrs. Greenhow made no effort to deny that she had acted as an agent to obtain information for the enemy. She proudly boasted that she had been able to get the plan for the Union advance and send it to Beauregard. She never revealed the source of this information, which included an exact copy of the orders issued to the army, but it must have come from some one in the confidence of the administration or army leaders.

For a number of months Mrs. Greenhow, together with a number of other women arrested as Confederate agents, were confined in the house on Sixteenth Street which was promptly called by the populace "Fort Greenhow." Many were the arguments I listened to as to what should be done with Mrs. Greenhow. Some were in favor of drastic measures; others thought her arrest and confinement had made her a heroine in the eyes of other women sympathetic to the South and that she ought to have been sent South immediately after her arrest. In January she was removed to the Old Capitol Prison and in May sent to Richmond. We never saw this fascinating spy again but were thrilled that she had found us worthy of cultivation.

At the beginning of the war it took patience and some stern military discipline to mold the civilian army into the compact, obedient machine which brought victory to the Union arms. These showy regiments of State militia had been the idols of their cities and always met with admiration when they paraded. When invited to attend a function in full dress uniform, they met in their armories and decided whether they would go or not.

When the Highlanders, in the reorganization which followed Bull Run, received orders to turn in their plaids and kilts and sporrans and dress in the regulation uniform of the army they were greatly angered, and simply exercising the well-known prerogative of American citizens, the inalienable right to knock the government and their temporary superiors, they held an indignation meeting and voted not to obey the order.

Things came to a head on August 14, 1861. That day my older brother, Surgeon Charles S. Taft, U. S. Signal Corps, burst into the house while we were at lunch, saying, "They're having a bad time with the Highlanders and two companies of regulars and a battery loaded with grape and canister are ordered out there. You'll see something you may never see again. Come quick!"

My father rose at once, and I slapped my big flat on my head and sped after him. "Oh, Charlie," I gasped, as I hurried to keep pace, "they will not use grape and canister! That scatters so and hits so many at once."

"If the artillerymen are ordered to fire, they will fire and so will the infantry. They are regulars, you know."

I knew, and as we hurried along I pictured those tall, proud Highlanders in their tartans, kilts and sporrans and bare knees, and remembered the splendid appearance they made in the "On to Richmond" advance of the month before, the bagpipes sounding a weird pibroch. As I remember, the camp of the Highlanders was not far from Kalorama, a beautiful place in the suburbs of Washington, afterwards taken by the government for a smallpox hospital.

We arrived just as two companies of regulars took up position on two sides of a square, the barracks being the third side, while on the fourth, in an open space, the rebellious soldiers were gathered, silent and sullen, their arms thrown in disorderly heaps upon the ground. Two companies of the highlanders which did not join the mutiny were drawn up a little to one side at parade rest. They had the fine regimental colors with them.

A gun of the battery clanked up, wheeled and jangled into position in the center of the line facing the open space, the artillerymen standing by, ready to serve.

We were standing a little distance back of the line of regulars near a group of officers, the colonel of the Highlanders and his staff. A mounted adjutant rode into the middle of the square. He took out his watch and holding it in his hand said, "You have five minutes, men, to take your arms and fall in. If you are not in line at the expiration of five minutes, the order will be given to fire."

As long as I live I shall see that young officer on his horse, motionless as a graven statue, his gold watch glittering in his hand and the lines of blue-coated regulars with still, set faces.

A long silence without stir or motion. I clutched my brother's arm and prayed, "O, Lord, make them give way. Make them give way." I did not pray to close the grinning mouth of that gun or that the line of regulars be held from firing. I knew better. If that quiet captain gave the order, I knew they would fire. My mind refused to think beyond that possibility.

"Steady, Sis, steady," whispered my brother. He told me afterwards that I pinched his arm black and blue. The colonel wiped the tears from his face with a handkerchief. The adjutant spoke again and his voice made us jump.

"You have two minutes to take up your arms and fall in before the order to fire is given."

A low order ran down the line of regulars, the muskets fell as one to the "aim" and we heard the click as they were cocked. But the recalcitrants began to pick up their arms and fall into line. Faster and faster the sergeants herded them into line. Thank God, it was over. The adjutant put up his watch and rode out, saluting the colonel as he passed. But a color guard from the regulars bore off the regimental colors, the beautiful flag. I cried a little then; it seemed cruel. But I was glad when, in a few months, I heard they had been given their colors back for gallantry in action.

This incident was kept out of the newspapers at the time. It would have hurt enlistments up North, but it remains in my memory as one of the vivid and heart-rending experiences of the war.

I was warned by my brother not to mention this mutiny of the Highlanders before President Lincoln. "He has enough to worry him," he said.

I was so impressed by the scene that it was hard for me to keep still about it, but I did, and I do not know whether he ever knew about it or not.

I heard some one tell my father that the President was very troubled by the number of desertions from General McClellan's army.

TEN

In the fall of 1861, Mrs. Lincoln had a desk and blackboard put into the end of the state dining room and secured a tutor for the boys. She asked my brothers to share his instruction as there were no schools open in Washington at this time. My father insisted on paying half the tutor's salary but Mrs. Lincoln said she had secured a place for him in one of the departments and he would spend his mornings there and teach the boys in the afternoon. The boys were doing well, though the younger pair were a little unruly, when my father suddenly lost his office.

It was found that some of his original backers were now in the Confederacy. I don't think father had considered this contingency, he was so busy looking after the soldiers. All his time out of office hours was spent in the hospitals and camps. I remember we had two convalescents at home with us at the time.

My father had an offer from Munn and Company at a higher salary, but President and Mrs. Lincoln did not wish the family to leave Washington. Mrs. Lincoln told my mother, "You must not go. We can't let you go."

The President wrote a strong letter asking my father's reinstatement. Came a bland answer expressing deep regret, but, alas, another man had been given the position. If the writer had only known how the President felt, etc., etc. Mrs. Lincoln wrote several letters which she sent with large bouquets. Finally the President gave up trying to cut the red tape that prevented my father's reinstatement and appointed him to another office. So we remained in Washington. It was perhaps about this time that Mr. Lincoln said he had "very little influence in this administration."

That fall we had several visits from an odd-looking Swedish gentleman named John Ericsson. My father told us that he was an inventor who had plans for constructing a new kind of warship which the government was considering. Father was considered an expert on steam engines; he had been in charge of the "steam room" in the Patent Office and may possibly have been delegated to pass on this part of Ericsson's new ship for the government. That "steam room" had an unholy fascination for Tad Lincoln, who wanted to play with the glistening little models of steam engines until finally my father had to lock them up in glass cases for protection. My father and Ericsson would argue for hours over large drawings and plans spread out on our dining-room table. Mr. Ericsson explaining in his slow Swedish accent and my father objecting in his quick way, "But your engines, man, your engines!"

Another month and we saw the Swedish inventor no more but we were told that his "crazy boat" was being built in a Long Island yard. And when finally, in March, this "crazy boat" defeated the *Merrimac,* my father got a great deal of satisfaction out of the report that the *Monitor's* engines had given trouble. "I told him his engines wouldn't do," he proclaimed triumphantly.

I remember well the thrill of terror which swept Washington when the news came that the *Merrimac* was out, for what was to prevent this strange monster, the first ironclad, from sailing up the river and shelling Washington. My father said Secretary Welles' white beard trembled as he told how the *Cumberland* sank with colors flying, firing her last gallant broadside as she went under. My father used to call Welles "the Old Man of the Sea" and said he didn't know which end of a ship went out first. All the cabinet were reported as frantic with fear, although President Lincoln seemed outwardly unmoved.

We were living then on Ninth Street, next door to Commodore Smith, whose son, Lieutenant Joseph Smith, commanded the *Congress,* stationed at Fortress Monroe. We were sitting on the porch when Commodore Smith passed on his way from the Navy Department where he had gone for news. In answer to a question from my father, he said brokenly, "Joe's dead. The *Congress* struck her flag." When my mother said something reassuring, the old sailor answered, "No, my boy would never surrender. If the flag's down, then Joe's dead." And Joe *was* dead, struck by a shell on the deck of his ship.

In the fall of 1861 I saw a good deal of the Lincoln family. My brothers were studying with the Lincoln boys under the tutor Mrs. Lincoln had provided and I was in and out of the White House almost every day.

One day Tad asked me to help him find his doll Jack. I went down to the sitting room and there was the President, stretched out in his large chair. His head was lying back, his eyes closed, his hands and feet extended, and such a worn and weary look upon his face that I closed the door softly and went back and told Tad, "Your father is just going to sleep and he is dreadfully tired. I saw Jack under his chair, but don't you dare disturb the President."

"Come on, Holly," said Tad gleefully, "let's go down just as still and give our Indian war whoop." They went down, as still as a load of bricks, and I heard their wild whoops below.

Late one afternoon I was curled up in the window of the sitting room, looking at a large book, when the President came in. I jumped to my feet.

He said, "How is Julie to-day? Sit down, child."

I was glad to do so for the book I was clasping was heavy. He took it from me, turned over the leaves absently, then put it on my lap, saying, "Such a big book for little Julie."

Resting one hand on my shoulder and the other on the window above my head, he looked long and earnestly over the Long Bridge into Virginia and sighed heavily. Then he walked up and down, up and down the long room, his hands behind him and his head bent, sighing now and then. I think he had entirely forgotten my presence. He looked so sad and worried that somehow I wanted to comfort him yet knew not how. And crying a little, I slipped out in the darkening twilight.

President Lincoln always appeared to me well dressed. I am sure I should have noticed otherwise, for I was a rather particular young person in regard to such things. And he never appeared awkward to me. My father was inclined to be critical in matters of etiquette but he said he never saw Lincoln embarrassed in greeting foreigners of distinction. "The President seems anxious to make every one comfortable and at their ease," remarked my father, "which is the essence of good breeding."

Once, as I was sitting on the sofa with some silk and velvet pieces on my lap, out of which I was trying to make a pin-cushion, the President came into the room. I rose at once, my pieces falling on the floor. When the President went out, I picked them up and was just getting them sorted out again when he came in the second time. True to my training, I again rose and the silk once more scattered to the floor.

"You needn't get up, Julia, every time Abram comes in the room," said Mrs. Lincoln.

"Why, Julie," said the President, noticing my silk pieces on the floor, "that's too bad." Before I knew what he was about, he had knelt on the floor and was picking up the pieces of silk for me. Greatly embarrassed at this presidential gallantry, I darted forward to help him and together we picked them up.

One day the boys and I, who should have known better, were leaning out of the front windows to watch a regiment go by, when the President passed and pulled us all in. He jerked in the boys with little ceremony but lifted me down gently, saying, "Do you want to break your neck, honey?"

Once I was sitting on the stairs reading when the President came down. I started to rise but he said, "Sit still, Julie. I'll walk right over you." Which he did, laughing at the joke, but telling me I had better go to the sitting room where the light was better. My mother had placed a ban on novels, so I devoured whatever I could find at the White House. Even there, however, I had no peace, for if Tad saw me he would report to my mother, "Julie was reading nobbel books at our house."

Another time I was in the sitting room with Mrs. Lincoln when the President came in with a bunch of photographs in his hand. They were new pictures of himself, and he and Mrs. Lincoln looked them over and commented on the different poses. Then he turned to me saying, "Julie, do you want my picture?"

"Oh, yes, sir," I said eagerly, for indeed I wanted one.

"Give me a kiss then and you can have it," he agreed. So I stretched up and he leaned over and I gave him a peck on the cheek. I remember to this day how scratchy his whiskers were.

He drew me to him, saying, "Now we will pick out a good one," and I still have the one we finally selected.

Whenever I think of Mr. Lincoln, I see him sprawled out in that big chair in the sitting room, for it was there that I came most in contact with him. I remember going to that room one morning rather early, looking for Mrs. Lincoln or the boys, and finding the President there alone in his big chair with the old, worn Bible on his lap. I crossed the room to bid him good morning. He spoke to me in an absent-minded sort of a way and clasping my hand, rested it on his knee, as I stood by him. He seemed to see something interesting out of the window. I stood there for what seemed to me a long time, with my hand clasped in his. I followed his gaze out of the window but could see nothing but the tops of some trees. I thought it wouldn't be polite for me to pull my hand out of his grasp, even if I could, so I stood there until my arm fairly ached. Why did I not ask him what he saw out there? I think he would have told me. Finally he turned to me with a look of startled surprise and said,

"Why, Julie, have I been holding you here all this time?" He released me and I went off to find the boys.

Willie Lincoln was very fond of my mother. One day at our house Tad was singing,

"Old Abe Lincoln a rail splitter was he,
And he'll split the Confederacee."

Willie asked, "Ought Tad to sing that song, Mrs. Taft? Isn't it real disrespectful to Pa?" My mother said she thought it rather bad taste for the President's son.

"Why, Mama Taft," said Tad. "Everybody in the world knows Pa used to split rails." He kicked the chair as he always did when reproved and added, "Well, I s'pose I can sing 'John Brown's Body.' "

Willie asked Bud, "Why do you call Pa Mr. President but you don't call Ma Mrs. President?"

"Oh," answered Bud, "it's not proper to call Presidents by their names. But your mother is just Mrs. Lincoln, only the servants call her the Madam."

Some one gave Willie a little watch charm and he presented it to me, saying, "I will give you my little gold dog, Julie, because I love you and you must keep it always." I accepted the gift, although I am afraid that at the time I did not reciprocate the sentiment that went with it. I was older than he and felt myself quite a grown-up young lady worthy of the attention of the attractively uniformed officers with which Washington abounded. But needless to say, I treasure Willie's gift now. Dear Willie, he was pure gold if the little dog was not.

I remember one occasion when Mrs. Lincoln had forbidden the boys to go with the President over the river to a review, as it was cold and windy and they all had bad colds. Just after the presidential cortege passed down the line, there came clattering after a cart drawn by a big, old, scraggly mule driven by a small, ragged, grinning darky, and bearing Willie and Bud and Tad and Holly with some old condemned swords somebody had given them held at salute. Willie said he and Bud hired the darky with some of their circus money.

About the limit in "letting the children have a good time," to quote Mrs. Lincoln's favorite phrase, was her permitting them to attend a state dinner. They sat near the foot of the table. My mother was properly shocked when Willie and Bud told her next day. The boys had stayed at the White House the night before because it rained.

"Why, Bud," said Mother, "did you even have fresh blouses?"

"Oh, yes," answered Bud. "You know you sent us a lot when we stayed with Willie and Tad the week their ma was in New York, and we put them in the drawer and now they are all mixed up and we don't know which is which."

"I've got on Bud's," said Willie proudly. "I know, 'cause it's tucks on the side. I told Ma when she took it out of the drawer, but she said never mind, it fitted me better than it did Bud and mine fitted him better."

I asked about the state dinner. "I tell you," boasted Tad, "those 'bassadors were all tied up with gold cords; they glittered grand."

Willie added, "Pa looked pretty plain with his black suit, but Ma was dressed up, you bet."

At the time the official notice of the death of the Prince Consort, the husband of Queen Victoria, came through the British minister, it was rumored in Washington society that Mrs. Lincoln intended to follow the example of European courts and put the "Republican Court" into ceremonial mourning, the women wearing purple dresses.

I do not know whether this was true. Every one thought it ridiculous but Mrs. Lincoln had two beautiful purple costumes, one a very regal purple velvet with white cord piping and buttons. The other was a rich silk. However, she wore a fine point lace shawl with the velvet gown and white roses in her hair, which certainly was not mourning.

Any one who knew her even slightly would know that she could not be kept waiting and not infrequently she was forced to wait on the President's movements when he was detained by some important business coming up suddenly. I remember well one evening of a levee. She was dressed for that occasion in a beautiful white satin with train and expansive hoops, flowers in her hair and even her white gloves on. She waited impatiently for a time for the President and then sent Willie to tell his father, who was in his private office, that it was time for them to appear at the levee. Willie came back, saying, "Pa is coming." After five minutes she said, "Bud, you go and tell Abe Lincoln if he don't come this instant I'll come for him." How Bud translated this impatient message into words proper for presidential ears I don't know, but in a few minutes he returned with the President, who was pulling on his large white gloves.

I always envied those gloves, they went on so easily and mine were so tight. When the President and Mrs. Lincoln appeared on the grand staircase the band struck up, "Hail to the Chief" and they went to their places while we followed unobtrusively.

ELEVEN

My half-brother, of whom I have spoken, was surgeon in charge of the Judiciary Square Hospital. I went there often to read to the soldiers, write letters for them or play cards with them. I wanted to be a regular nurse but Miss Dix, who was head of the nurses, told me she never took any under thirty years of age. My brother would not have any women nurses in his hospital. He used convalescent soldiers and medical students for such work. Doctor Mary Walker wanted to be taken on his staff but he had a horror of her because she wore men's clothes. I knew her quite well, though her natty men's suits always gave me a pain.

The President and Mrs. Lincoln visited the hospital quite often, bringing fruit and flowers, and Charlie said it always cheered the men. Mr. Lincoln wrote to Hiram Barney in New York:

"Mrs. Lincoln has $1000 for the benefit of the hospitals and she will be obliged and send the pay if you will be so good as to select and send her $200 worth of good lemons and $100 worth of good oranges."

Mrs. Lincoln distributed this fruit to the different hospitals and Judiciary Square had its share.

After the great battles the loads of wounded were more than the hospitals in Washington could accommodate. After one battle I remember ambulances were unloaded in the courthouse square on the soft turf, a few men wrapped in blankets, some propped up against the wall of Judiciary Square Hospital.

My brother and his assistants sorted them out. He told my father to get the names and home addresses of one group he said could not last long; it was hardly worth while to get cots for them. An officer leaning against the wall to whom my father spoke, answered sharply, "I do not care to give you my address." When my father returned in two hours, the officer had been taken away dead.

I was sent to a carpenter shop near by where the slightly wounded were put. Two girls I knew were there and we carried bowls of soup with bread and coffee to the men. They were lying or sitting on straw and shavings. In the entry between the room used as a kitchen and the one where the men were I noticed a man propped in the corner behind a door, who was apparently unconscious. His head was covered with blood from a saber cut over the temple. As I passed through, carrying some dishes to the kitchen, a surgeon touched my arm. "Get some water and wash that man off," he ordered. "I'll send an orderly to bring him to me to have his cut dressed."

I brought water and a rag and began. I turned faint and sick and went to the open door for air. When my sight cleared I went back and washed some more but I had to go to the fresh air three times more before I finished him. The last time his eyes were open and he murmured, "Wot in 'ell," but the orderly came just then, picked him up and took him to the place where the surgeon was.

The sight of blood has never turned me faint since. It was a complete cure.

Adjutant Jones was an English soldier with a medal from the Crimea who was brought to my brother's hospital with his leg shattered below the knee. Amputation seemed necessary but he suddenly produced a pistol, which in some way he had managed to conceal, and in a cold voice announced, "If any of you sawbones tries to cut off my leg I'll shoot you." My brother told him of the danger of gangrene. "I'll risk it," he answered and he was left because my brother said he could not expose the whole ward to a disturbance. They watched for him to fall asleep but he did not. The nurse even tried to throw a spray of chloroform over him but he held a newspaper before him and threatened to shoot if the attempt was repeated. The third day there were no symptoms of gangrene and the upshot of it all was that Adjutant Jones saved his leg and when I last saw him was walking with one cane instead of two crutches, which was the best I expected.

I remember one day telling the President about reading to the soldiers in my brother's hospital and he asked, "Does it make you sad, seeing all those wounded men?"

I answered, "Yes, and I think everybody will be sad until the war is over."

"Yes, Julie," he said. "I think they will."

I came to the White House one afternoon and found the family in a state of nervous tension on account of the absence of Tad and Holly Taft who had left immediately after breakfast and had not returned. My two brothers had stayed all night with the Lincoln boys. Willie and Bud had spent the morning on the flat roof, which they had rigged up as the deck of a ship, giving orders and looking for "enemy cruisers" through an old spyglass. They came down for lunch but the other two were missing. I reported that they had not been seen at our house. Servants were sent in various directions in vain and the anxiety grew until shortly after dark when the two boys arrived home with a gentleman who brought them in his carriage. He said that a workman had heard the boys calling in the Capitol vaults and had led them out. They had been lost in those vast dark places all day.

Tad said, "A man who knew Pa gave us some dinner in the restaurant." After that they got the idea of seeing how far down they could go in the Capitol. They knew the way around the ordinary places but had never been in the sub-basement. "We went down steps pretty near to China," Holly explained, "and when there weren't any more steps to go down, Tad dared me to explore around and we did and got lost."

Tad said, "We knew there couldn't be any bears there, but there were rats and it was awful dark." It really was a precarious adventure for a couple of boys.

I was in the Capitol grounds with my father when the top of the great Statue of Liberty was swung into place by the big crane and carefully adjusted to its place. Just when the fastenings were pulled away a white dove, one of a flock which were always around the Capitol grounds, circled around the head of the statue and finally lighted there. It was seen by many people in the grounds and "a sign of peace" was in many mouths. My father said to me. "You must tell the President."

It was said that Mrs. Lincoln believed in signs but the President believed in dreams. There was one dream he told his friends he always had before every great battle—before Bull Run, Antietam, Chancellorsville, Gettysburg—always the same dream: that of a ship sailing swiftly over strange waters to a dark shore. He had that dream the night before he was assassinated but he did not interpret it as a warning to himself. To some friends who were looking for news from Sherman he said, "I had my dream last night and we will have news soon from the army." And he went out on that last drive with his wife in joyous spirits. She said he was more cheerful than he had been since the death of Willie and they talked happily of the years before them. The war was over, they would enjoy life now. This was Pisgah to this Moses who had led his people through the dreadful wilderness of battle and death. This was his look into the Promised Land he was not to enter. At this hour the dream was not interpreted and his habitual sadness was lightened.

Not long before he had had a still more sinister dream. He told his wife and Mr. Lamon, his former law partner about it. He said, "It was deathly still in my dream, but I heard sounds of weeping. I went through the house and came to the East Room where I saw a coffin and a guard of soldiers round it. I asked, 'Who is dead?' They said, 'The President has been assassinated.'"

He should have had a guard, in the box at Ford's theater that fatal night and another stationed outside.

Mrs. Lincoln always laughed at her husband's premonitions. But Lincoln knew. His prescient soul saw it somewhere, somehow, sometime ahead, but perhaps on that one happy day he was permitted to enjoy, the dream faded, the vision was not with him.

I have often been asked what I thought about Mr. Lincoln's religion. At the time I knew him I do not think it ever entered my head to wonder about his religion, one way or the other. In that day people took their religion seriously and defended strenuously the tenets of the particular creed they professed. Some men in public life were openly agnostic and rather gloried in their disbelief. A few, like my father, went through the forms of conventional religion with certain rather heretical reservations which they kept mostly to themselves. I remember my father once giving a natural explanation of one of the Bible miracles and my mother's shocked protest, "Horatio, you will turn the children into infidels."

The fact that Mr. Lincoln was not a church member bothered some people. "He might just as well join," remarked a neighbor of ours, "and it would set a better example." My mother said she understood he came near joining the Baptist church when a young man and the neighbor replied, "Well, if that's the case, it's just as well be didn't." The neighbor was a Presbyterian with no great liking for Baptists.

Back in that day many families conducted some sort of family worship. It was considered the proper thing by families who had a definite church connection but I do not remember that the Lincoln family did, although both the President and his wife were scrupulous in most of the outward observances of religion and attended church regularly. I remember, too, that when Willie died they sent for Doctor Gurley, their pastor.

It is well known, of course, that Mr. Lincoln was a great reader of the Bible, but I have a notion, without knowing exactly why I have it, that at the beginning of the war he read the Bible quite as much for its literary style as he did for its religious or spiritual content. Perhaps I have this notion from his attitude when reading it. He read it in the relaxed, almost lazy attitude of a man enjoying a good book. There is a good deal on record about his being a man of prayer but I never heard him pray or saw him in the attitude of prayer, although I have seen him in moods when he might well have been struggling in silent prayer.

Only once do I recall his saying anything about the Bible or religion and that was in reply to Tad's plea as to why he had to go to Sunday-school. "Every educated person should know something about the Bible and the Bible stories, Tad," answered his father.

That answer struck me as odd. It was not the conventional reason for attending Sunday-school but I have thought since that it summed up the most useful result from attending Sunday-school in that day. We got a deal of creed and moral reflections, most of which have been forgotten. But the Bible stories still stick.

TWELVE

Saturday morning, at our house, was devoted to a study of the Sunday-school lesson. Willie and Tad appeared early, as they always did, when Bud and Holly did not appear early at the White House. The Lincoln boys had enrolled themselves with my brothers in the Sunday-school of our church, the Fourth Presbyterian, and Mrs. Lincoln had expressed to my mother her pleasure that they were learning their lessons and hoped we "would encourage them to keep on."

To sister Julia had been intrusted the not altogether pleasant duty of inculcating a reasonable working knowledge of two pages of the blue question book, while she embroidered a ruby velvet watchcase, which was to be Bud's Christmas present to some idolized officer.

It was December and cold. Willie and Tad had been talking of winters in Illinois, of skating and sledding and snow-balling. My Washington-bred brothers listened with round eyes. They possessed no mittens, no sled, no skates. They had never known the delights of a real snow-storm. Perhaps Washington was farther south before the war, because in the time I lived there, very few were the occasions when enough snow was on the ground to justify the appearance even for an hour of the nondescript creations known in the capital as sleighs.

Tad dashed at the Sabbath questions with the cheerful audacity characteristic of him. Willie sighed as he said that there were "more hard words than ever in it." He and Bud debated whether their teacher would require them to have it perfect or would "let them off easy on the names."

The very youngest son of the family, Willie Taft, being what Tad called a "Sunday-school infant" and not required to study any lesson, sat curled up on the window seat, where, by craning his neck, he could see a bit of the square, the barracks, and the end of the guard-house with Sentry Number 1 appearing and disappearing with clocklike regularity.

The older boys studied with set, determined looks. There were several bits of catechism deftly interpolated; and in our Sunday-school these must be recited verbatim. Tad and Holly wriggled and fidgeted, repeating the lines in a loud whisper, each gradually departing from the text and copying the other's mistakes until they had to begin all over again.

The infant scholar in the window also diverted attention by proclaiming at intervals, "There's a dwunk man walking the beat with a log," or "Here comes the officer of the day; they're turning out the guard." Again it would be, "I fink there's a hundred army mules up the street fighting right smart."

Tad paused in the murmur of "the moral law—the moral law—" to ask, "Julie, what is a mud sill?"

"Never mind, Tad, go on. 'The moral law is summarily comprehended—' "

"But, what is it?"

"Why, a Yankee, Tad."

"Well, a boy in Lafayette Square said we were 'em and we am not."

"Of course not," said Willie Lincoln. "Everybody knows they come from Connecticut."

"Bud and Willie wouldn't let me punch him 'cause they said it would be put in the papers, but I will if he says it again."

It was still cold and wet and blustering. Only an occasional officer rode past, his great cape over his head, followed by a dejected orderly. The boys watched the gusts of rain anxiously. They had been promised a ride with the staff if it was not too stormy.

My cousin, a tall young captain from "Camp Desolation," came and leaned against the doorway and sympathetically confessed that he himself had to learn the Commandments and Creed before the morrow's morn.

"What for?" demanded the boys, astonished that the shoulder-strapped six-footer should still be in thralldom to the blue question book.

"Because we have a Sunday-school in the defenses, and mind you, the colonel is superintendent. I never saw anything in the army regulations," the captain complained, "about having to drill the men in the Bible as well as the manual of arms."

"Snow! snow!" shouted Tad, as some light flakes flew by the window. "That's what I like better'n anything. I hope it'll be over the fences."

Tad's wish was futile. To his great disappointment the snowflakes grew more and more infrequent, and at last the sun shone out. The boys went off, hopeful of a ride at least.

About noon a relative arrived unexpectedly. As he had to go to his command that evening and wished to see the children, I was sent to find the boys and bring them home. I went at once to the White House and looked outside first; the grounds, the stable, the conservatory; then the kitchen, where I learned that the boys had an early lunch and had not been seen since. The ride with the staff had not materialized and the Madam had gone for a drive but had not taken the boys.

I ran up into the sitting room and almost collided with the tall form of the President, who was crossing the room on the way to his office. He had some papers in one hand and with the other he stopped my flight, saying, "Here, here, flibbertigibbet, where are you going in such a hurry?"

"I am looking for the boys and I cannot find them anywhere. Cousin Sam Andrus is at our house with a colonel. I forget his name but he is awfully nice."

"Awfully nice, is he?" said Mr. Lincoln, with the quizzical smile I remember so well.

"Yes, sir, and they want to see the boys, ours and yours, Willie and Tad, you know."

"Yes, I know. Have you looked in the attic, Julie?"

"I'm going there now," I said, and left him watching my headlong progress toward the attic, with that same smile on his face.

In the attic was a large bin of visiting cards, which apparently had been lately disturbed, as there was a nest hollowed out in the center, and the cards were scattered all around the floor. But the boys were not there; so I went home and reported.

After dinner, as the men were enjoying their cigars on the veranda, the four boys appeared, dragging a remarkable object which consisted mainly of an old chair on barrel staves and the cover of a Congressional Record nailed to the broken seat. This, they proudly informed us, was a snow sled.

Holly hung back as they were severally presented to the colonel, and Tad triumphantly explained that "Holly burned an awful hole in his pants with powder out of a cartridge given him by a soldier who said it wouldn't go off."

Both Tad and Holly were very uneasy and continually rubbed against the veranda railing. When questioned by mother, Tad said, "I s'pose it's the snowballs we've got down our backs."

"Snowballs," said mother, surprised. "Where did you find any snow?"

"Up in our attic," said Tad. "Handfuls and handfuls and bushels and bushels."

Naturally we all looked amazed at this statement until Willie explained. "Why, Mama Taft, Tad's snow is cards. There are bushels in our attic in a big bin and we throw them up and play it's snowing. There are all the cards all the people have left on the Presidents since General Washington."

"General Washington never lived in your house," said Bud. "The tutor said he didn't."

"Well, there's enough to make a snowstorm without his," said Willie.

"And Tad and Holly stuffed them down each other's backs like real snow, but I guess they're sharp-cornered and sticky."

"Yes," said Tad; "they stick to you and they stick into you."

Declaring they couldn't stand it another minute, Holly and Tad went upstairs, Tad calling back, "Next time we'll pour the snow on the attic stairs and slide down on our snow sled."

The next morning, going into the boys' room, I saw in the middle of the card-strewn floor the name of Jenny Lind, the great singer. So I picked up this card, and then another and another, as they interested me, leaving many to be swept up by the maid.

And here are some snowflakes from Tad Lincoln's snowstorm.

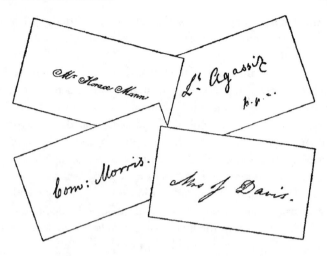

In February, 1862, Fort Foote, on the Potomac River halfway between Washington and Mount Vernon, went into commission with an
imposing military ceremony. The boys of the Ninth New York Heavy
Artillery, of which my cousin, Colonel Eward P. Taft, was commander,
had worked for months on the fort. My father and I went down the day
before and were the guests of my cousin and his wife who with their
three children had lived at the fort all winter in log barracks.

Colonel William H. Seward, Jr., son of the Secretary of State, was in
charge of the ceremonies, formally putting the fort into commission and
he invited me to pull the lanyard of the big gun when it was discharged
for the first time. Of course I was delighted to take so important a part
in the day's program. With the regiment at dress parade, I was escorted
by the officer of the day to an elevated position beside the big gun. The
captain put the lanyard in my hand, stuffed some cotton in my ears
and warned me to rise on tiptoe and open my mouth when I pulled
the cord.

"Now, Julia," he said, "when the band plays, 'Oh, say can you see,'
pull the cord. Pull the cord on 'See.'"

I waited. The bugles blew, the band struck up, "Oh, say can you
see—and I pulled the cord. Heaven and earth seemed to come together
in one grand crash as the great gun rolled back in the recoil. The soldiers

presented arms, a long line of cavalry saluted with glittering sabers, the Stars and Stripes rose slowly to the top of the flagpole and Fort Foote was in commission.

The next day the ladies of the fort had a picnic at Mount Vernon, which during the war was kept neutral. We had a fine day and I was allowed to whirl Martha Washington's spinning wheel and sit on George's bed. But just as an old darky fiddler appeared and we thought of a dance under the colonnade, with about twenty-five officers, six married ladies as chaperons and one girl, word was brought that a man had been seen to saddle a horse and ride into the woods. So we were hustled down into our boat, and just in time too, to escape Early and his greycoats whom we saw in the woods. The two orderlies who had stayed behind to bring the lunch baskets down to the landing were captured and spent two years in Libby prison.

In that month came the dreadful blow of Willie Lincoln's death. In his illness he called for Bud, and my brother was with him most of the time.

The President would come in and stand awhile at the bedside, then go out without speaking. Once he laid his arm across Bud's shoulder and stroked Willie's hair. It was late and he said, "You ought to go to bed, Bud."

Bud answered, "If I go he will call for me."

One of the servants told my mother that the President, coming in later, picked up Bud, who had fallen asleep, and carried him tenderly to bed.

About noon of February twentieth my mother brought word from the White House that Willie had held Bud's hand and seemed better. He died at five o'clock.

Mrs. Lincoln wrote to my mother, "Please keep the boys home the day of the funeral; it makes me feel worse to see them." The President, however, sent for Bud to see Willie before he was put in the casket. Bud had to be carried from the room and was ill for some days after.

My mother naturally waited for some word from Mrs. Lincoln before allowing us to go to the White House. But the word never came and shortly after she took us North to put us in school.

I was in Washington the winter of 1864 and attended with my sister-in-law one of Mrs. Lincoln's Saturday afternoon receptions. On the way

Sallie told of going with a committee of Washington ladies to Willard's to present a basket of flowers to the new commander, General Grant. They sent up a card to his room and waited a long time, then questioned the call boy who said:

"Yes'm, I done give de card to de gen'ril, and he done went down de back stairs and get on his hoss and went to camp."

Mrs. Lincoln seemed glad to see me again and was quite her old affectionate self, asking after my mother and the family. But when Tad came in and saw me, he threw himself down in the midst of the ladies and kicked and screamed and had to be taken out by the servants.

Mrs. Lincoln said, "You must excuse him, Julia. You know what he remembers." It was a very painful scene and I never saw Mrs. Lincoln or Tad again.

I was not in Washington at the time Lincoln was shot. My brother, Surgeon Charles Sabin Taft, was in the theater that night and when he heard the shot and saw Booth, whom he knew well, he sensed what had occurred. Climbing over the orchestra he was assisted up into the box the same way Booth had come down. He was the first surgeon to reach the President and he told me afterwards that at the first examination he was sure the wound was mortal. He took the President's head in his arms and assisted by several men they carried Lincoln out of the theater and across the street to the house where he later died.

Until the Surgeon General and the President's family physician arrived, my brother was in charge. Colonel Oldroyd, in his book, "The Assassination of Lincoln," says that Colonel Taft stood at the head of the dying President all that dreadful night, controlling the flow of blood from the wound with his finger.

He received orders from the Surgeon General to report to the artist for the official picture of the "Deathbed of Lincoln." That picture can be seen in the house on Tenth Street where Lincoln died, in Colonel Oldroyd's museum of Lincoln relics. In the picture my brother is shown standing at the head of the bed with his hands on Lincoln's head.

Several days after, he found in the pocket of the coat he wore that night Lincoln's collar and tie and some wisps of hair he had cut off on his first examination. These he turned over to the Surgeon General. The yard of the house where Lincoln died was full of blossoming lilacs, and as long as Charlie Taft lived the scent of lilacs would turn

The Death Bed of Lincoln
From the genuine official copy

him sick and faint, as it brought back the black horror of that dreadful night.

He knew Booth well and was one of those called to identify the body before it was buried under a stone slab in the old jail. I remember John Wilkes Booth as a handsome, jolly young man who would pull my long curls. He was buried at night, my brother said. Afterwards the body was given to Edwin Booth and now lies in an unmarked grave in a Baltimore cemetery.

Mrs. Lincoln was not fitted to withstand a violent blow to her emotions. If she gave herself up to such abandon of grief on the death of her young son that she would not allow the Marine Band to give their usual weekly concerts on the White House grounds for so long that Mr. Lincoln had to countermand her order, and she could not stand even the sight of Willie's playmates, what would be the result of the awful shock which shook the whole world when President Lincoln, her husband, was assassinated?

What could one expect but that, stunned at first by the suddenness and horror of it, she literally went wild with sorrow. I do not believe her mind ever fully recovered its poise.

Before Mrs. Lincoln left Washington, my father was calling at the White House and Mrs. Lincoln gave him a funeral badge which she said had been sent to her by the silk weavers of Lyons, France. It is a beautiful piece of silk weaving and I count it among my chief treasures. At the top are these words, "I have said nothing but what I am willing to live by and if it be the pleasure of Almighty God, to die by. A. Lincoln." Then the eagle with the motto, E Pluribus Unum, in its beak, and perched on a shield surmounting a picture of Lincoln in a star-shaped frame. Under the picture "The Late Lamented President Lincoln." All of the letters and the picture are woven and are as clear as a photograph.

These are my girlhood memories of Tad Lincoln's father. Slight and trifling they seem, but "these little truthful stories simply told" may cast a ray of human softness over the sad, stern face of that great Servant of the Lord, who was among us unrecognized, lonely, sad, uncomforted, save as seeing Him who is invisible.

THE END

Index